A LETTER TO THE CHURCH AND THE NEXT GENERATION

SPIRITUAL GROWTH THROUGH THE WITNESS OF JAMES

ENDORSEMENTS

Robin's deep commitment to the Lord, heartfelt passion for the truth, and genuine love for the next generation spill across every page. Combining solid scholarship with Spirit-led insight, *A Letter to the Church* provides a springboard for transformation and spiritual growth for mentor and mentee alike. An exceptional resource!

—Liz Curtis Higgs, author, Director of Spiritual Formation, Christ Church United Methodist, Louisville, Kentucky

This book arrives with God's perfect timing. Church abandonment by the young is at an all-time high. Multigenerational mentoring and deep discipleship have become, sadly, a lost art. The Rev. Robin Jennings draws insightfully upon the wisdom of James to create this readable, valuable, and biblically-rooted resource for Christian mentors working with young adults and emerging leaders.

—John W. Kyle, **PhD.** Executive National Director, The Fellows Initiative

There's nothing more fascinating than uncovering the texture of relationships by digging into the barely seen layers that lie beneath the words on the pages out of the Bible. Robin Jennings has for a long time been thoughtfully excavating his way around the Letter of James, and what emerges is a fascinating depiction of James's role as a spiritual mentor in the first century Jerusalem church.

Jennings then shows us how this story of mentoring can enrich our next generation for the church here and now.
—The Rev. Richard Kew, St. George's Episcopal Church, Nashville, Tennessee, author, *Vision Bearers: Dynamic Evangelism in the 21st Century*

From his own experience as a young Episcopal priest and pastor, the Rev. Robin Jennings shares his experience and love of Christ with his readers. Recognizing the need to walk with a spiritual mentor, Robin encourages us to be such a guide by providing direction, not in isolation, but within the context of the multi-generational church community. As we come out of the pandemic, rather than despair, Jennings identifies young disciples who are resilient and who are bouncing back with hope and are looking for just a little bit of help from those who have gone before them. This book provides encouragement for all ages to interact with God and one another as we grow spiritually with James and "count it all joy."
—The Rt. Rev. W. Michie Klusmeyer, Bishop of West Virginia

The Rev. Robin Jennings writes cogently about what should be the church's most pressing concern: the need for spiritual mentors to shepherd the youngest generation—a generation which is overloaded with *information* but starved for *formation*. He holds up James, the "living link to Jesus," as an example of one of these mentors, speaking from ages ago to the youth of today out of his own Spirit-fueled wisdom. What Jennings finds in James is a call to maturity, recommitment, and renewal on the part of Christians seeking to walk alongside today's young people and guide them to the life-giving way of Christ. A must-read for all those who are willing to lay the necessary spiritual foundation of growth for our children today and who desire a bright future for the church tomorrow.
—Karen Ellestad, chaplain, Episcopal Day School, Augusta, Georgia

Robin Jennings is passionate about the church of Jesus and its vitality in this secular age. In *A Letter to the Church and the Next Generation* Jennings focuses his passion on the urgent need for 'spiritual mentors' in the church to shepherd young adults toward spiritual maturity, using the often-neglected Epistle of James as his guide. Always practical, this study will greatly benefit anyone who shares Jennings's passion for the next generation of disciples and the church they inherit.

—**Steve Jester**, pastor, Second Presbyterian Church, Louisville, KY

Our organization has been blessed to benefit from Robin Jennings's vision for serving the next generation. With his help, the Imagination Library has demonstrated remarkable results – connecting with caring adults who are willing to slow down and read to children. Robin offers a similar model here by encouraging spiritual mentors to slow down and share wisdom from the church for young adults who seek deeper meaning for today.

—**Bill Shory**, Board President, Co-founder Imagination Library of Louisville, Inc.

The epistle of James proposes "orthopraxy" that is a salve for our age of duplicity, division and many social challenges, and I know of no better priest and pastor to serve as a guide than the Rev. Robin Jennings. This book is full of pastoral wisdom, practical insights, and spiritual nourishment. Trust me—this book will yield rich study and contemplation.

—**The Rev. Clint Wilson**, rector, St. Francis in the Fields, Harrods Creek, Ky.

A LETTER TO THE CHURCH AND THE NEXT GENERATION

SPIRITUAL GROWTH THROUGH THE WITNESS OF JAMES

Robin T. Jennings

ELK LAKE PUBLISHING INC

PUBLISHING THE POSITIVE
Plymouth, Massachusetts

COPYRIGHT NOTICE

PUBLISHED BY: Elk Lake Publishing, Inc., 35 Dogwood Drive, Plymouth, MA 02360, 2021

Library Cataloging Data

Names: Jennings, Robin T. (Robin T. Jennings)

A Letter to the Church and the Next Generation / Robin T. Jennings

202 p. 23cm × 15cm (9in × 6 in.)

Identifiers: ISBN-13: 978-1-64949-437-5 (paperback) | 978-1-64949-438-2 (trade hardcover) | 978-1-64949-439-9 (trade paperback) | 978-1-64949-440-5 (e-book)

Key Words: James Bible Commentary; spiritual mentor; vocational discernment; Christian faith book; life transitions book; calling; Book of James

Library of Congress Control Number: 2021950271 Nonfiction

DEDICATION

To the next generation,
And especially our grandchildren,
Janie, Will, Catherine, Annie, Mary Frances, and Henry
May You Be Doers of the Word

TABLE OF CONTENTS

ACKNOWLEDGMENTS

As I finish this manuscript and prepare to submit it, I am brought back to how the book you are holding began. It started at St. Francis in the Fields Episcopal Church with my teaching a Bible study on James. The class was a large one. I would present in lecture format followed by the class breaking into small groups for further discussion. What I still remember was the energy in the room and the inspiration and spirit James—not I—provided for all in attendance. Apparent to me was the Letter of James was speaking to the class in a way that was beyond me. It was like sailing and just letting the wind blow. Thank you to Kathy Foster and Marianne Reutlinger who organized this class, and of course, all the small group leaders and those who participated—know of my deep appreciation.

But this is not where the story ended. After the class concluded for the year, I put my notes away and was ready to move on. Some who participated in the class, however, were not through. They wanted more. Not more of me. But more of James. Interest in being "doers of the word" and what that looked like and meant took hold for many in the parish. The Table of Contents, in fact, actually began to take shape with the disciplines and practices James identifies as they became embedded in my preaching and teaching but more importantly in the parish ministry. I no longer was a teacher but more a mentor.

One example of the class on James came in our partnership and yoking with Pastor Anthony Middleton and the good people of Cable Baptist Church in Louisville. Cable Baptist is a lively, predominately Black American parish with a storied tradition and involvement with the Underground Railroad. The Ohio River, which is nearby their church, was like the River Jordan—especially for those seeking to break free the shackles derived from slavery during the period of the Civil War.

I mention this because Louisville struggles, like many cities, with racial strife. Our fervent desire was for the two churches to avoid divisive distinctions in the body of Christ and to practice congregational care for one another, which is as timely today as it was with James and the church in Jerusalem.

Of course, the recent pandemic kept us all socially isolated. Although it did provide me with quiet and solitude for writing, I confess the way of Zoom nearly became a way of life. I did, however, find Cathy Fyock, who is nationally known book coach and author, in Louisville. For me, she is so much more. Cathy encouraged me to expand my teaching and writing to include speaking. Her connections with the National Speakers Association allowed me to meet regularly on Zoom conference calls with a like-minded group, who provided both the encouragement and the strategic thinking as we planned our lives after the pandemic. Paul Elway, Claire Biedenharn, Jenny Smith, and the Rev. Elizabeth Stone all brought to the screen their own unique gifts and competencies as we worked on our writing while planning our speaking.

Stephanie Feger continues to provide enthusiastic support and solid guidance both with her marketing ideas and as my publicist. She is the one who has brought me out from under a rock into the light of day with social media and blogging. As a result, Stephanie has helped me build a foundation for a platform which I can grow for years to come. I have already seen remarkable results from her efforts, and there is no way I could have done any of this without her.

The list of acknowledgments continues but what you hold in your hand is a real team effort. Tracy Crump spent countless hours with me as a line editor—meaning she did most of the heavy lifting in bringing this manuscript into a readable format. As a fellow author, she was juggling her schedule and release of her new book while making room to help me into my production phase.

Here Deb Haggerty with Elk Lake Publishing came into the picture. Wouldn't you know Deb's formal signature reminds us to "count it all joy," which is of course, straight from the Letter of James (James 1:2). Call this partnership "good luck," but I would prefer to think of it as more providential in the way her publishing company works and what they expect from their authors. Thank you, Deb, Susan K. Stewart, and all at Elk Lake. What a wonderful group you have assembled, and I am so pleased to join you.

As always, I turn to my wife Mary who has been my constant pillar of support. I use the word "pillar" intentionally, since James was described by Paul as an acknowledged "pillar of faith" (Galatians 2:9). I think it then only appropriate in my acknowledgements to consider my wife in this same light. Being a writer is not easy, especially after a day completing only a few sentences and a paragraph. Suffice it to say, all the more difficult is being the spouse and asking, "How did it go today?" Mary was sincere in her asking and for her patience in listening and support in my writing. I want her to know of my love which "bears all things" especially with her as my pillar.

You will find in the dedication we have grandchildren who represent the next generation, but who are as well a reminder of the importance found in the gift of family life. James bore witness to this life, and he provides spiritual direction for us today as we are called into "doing the word" for the church tomorrow.

Robin T. Jennings
Louisville, Kentucky

INTRODUCTION

This is a book written and designed for spiritual mentors who are called to serve the next generation. Writing a job description is important. Of greater importance is identifying and recruiting those interested in filling such a position. The church needs the necessary gifts, skills, and competencies for spiritual mentors already found in grandparents, parents, aunts, and uncles. Godparents, role models, adults with faith in Christ, and all who have not given up on this next generation are vital. Spiritual mentors are not new. In the empty tomb and the resurrection, James provides this witness and the call for spiritual mentors now. The church and the next generation have heard enough. It's time to do the Word. The witness of James addresses this need today.

Full disclosure—the church has always been important in my life. The church taught me the meaning of love. Christian love, called *agápē* in Greek, translates as self-giving, sacrificial, the highest form of love. The sacrament of marriage further instilled within me this greater understanding of love, as did baptism and having four children. Paying for our boys to go to college almost killed me, but the experience reminded me how words like sacrament, sacrifice, and sacred are all interrelated.

As an adult, I saw life and religion, church and family, work and home interwoven and bound together. This may seem typical for an ordained minister, yet I can still recall applying to seminary the summer my wife and I planned to get married. The dean of the seminary, the director of admissions, my bishop—everyone seemed to say, "Wait." As you know, the last thing a young adult wants to hear is the word, "wait."

I was young and impatient. My wife, Mary, and I married in July and went off to seminary in August. Our marriage revolved from then on around the church. Granted, we knew little about other jobs, careers, or competing vocations. Church became our life and shaped our marriage. And I was part of the new generation.

After graduating from seminary, I accepted my first assignment to serve at St. Mary's Cathedral in Memphis, Tennessee. St. Mary's fit the picture of a grand old cathedral and had a wonderful history of being focused on doing God's work. As a young priest in the Episcopal church, I found my faith reinforced by worship there. The music, the splendid architecture, the liturgy—all were transcendent for a brand new clergyman. The ritual stirred me, and even though my ministry at St. Mary's was my first real job, it hardly seemed like work at all. I was pumped up, and I discovered something, kneeling in front of the altar week in and week out.

There my mind caught hold of an inscription on the marble steps where I knelt. Dedicated to the Sisters of St. Mary, 1878, is an inscription that simply reads: "Alleluia Osanna." At some point, I found the nerve to inquire what the inscription meant. With rapt attention, I was told and listened to the many stories of the selfless service given by Constance and her companions.

With devotion and remarkable energy, Constance led a small band of Anglican nuns to minister and care for residents living in the neighborhood district of the cathedral during the virulent spread of the yellow fever epidemic of 1878. Working out of the cathedral, the nuns and several priests moved among homes of the sick and dying. They gathered orphans and the widows and cared for all who were within their reach. Citizens who fled left only an estimated twenty thousand residents remaining in Memphis during the epidemic, and the death rate exceeded eighty a day in the summer, rising even higher in the fall. These are brutal statistics for any time. For Memphis, a city only beginning to recover from the Civil War, the death toll turned the community into a ghost town. Sadly, for the genteel Southern people living there, the epidemic reduced a once-proud city into a den of looting, murder, and insanity.[1]

On September 9, 1878, the Mother Superior, Sister Constance, died from the yellow fever at the age of thirty-three. Her last words were, "Alleluia! Osanna!" translated from Latin as "Give praise to the Lord." From being transcribed on marble steps at the foot of the altar to being inscribed upon my heart, the words often caused me to leave worship with a deeper and more profound understanding of the church. Constance and her companions reinforced my idealism as the call to praise the Lord was not lip service, but church service.

Shortly after we moved from Memphis to Louisville in 1981, the Episcopal Church began setting aside the day of September 9 in the calendar of Feasts and Fasts to commemorate the memory of the Sisters of St. Mary, The Martyrs of Memphis. This impression of the cathedral was now making a lasting mark.

Fast-forward to COVID-19. The memory of Constance echoes from the past and resonates today. As a result, there is a fervent desire within me to hand off this legacy of the church vocation, attributes, and witness to the next generation. But young adults today are missing from church. Religious conflicts, social upheaval, differing worldviews, and technology all seem to pile on and become deterrents to active church involvement. I wondered about the spiritual landscape young adults face today and how it differs from the forces boomers of my generation encountered, or the 1878 church in Memphis, or more especially the first century Jerusalem church begun by James.

This inquiry brought awareness of the call for church vocation, unique church attributes, and a necessary witness of the church mission. The point person is a spiritual mentor—a caring adult, who hears the Word and reaches out to the next generation.

The first chapter in the Letter of James provides both an introduction and a framework for the Christian community to engage in this discussion. In addition, the Barna Group has done extensive research that reinforces and strengthens the need for the church to not count this next generation out. Both James and Barna are writing for a small group of resilient young disciples who are capable of restoring the world here on earth, just as it is in heaven. My invitation is to simply hold James in one hand and Barna research in the other while reading this book— a juggling act, granted. But this is what the next generation requires. They also need you—not as an acquaintance at coffee hour, but you as a spiritual mentor.

YOU LOST ME

Years ago, I became acquainted with David Kinnaman of the Barna Group. Backed with extensive research, thousands of interviews, and solid study of both the church and young adults, David has written several books on how the church needs to equip young adults with a faith that both serves them and helps them serve. The title of one, published in 2011, almost says it all: *You Lost Me*. The book addresses young adults and the consequences of a church maintaining status quo. In the end, it encourages and calls for intergenerational thinking as does the Letter of James. Imbedded in both writings is a simple message: Christian spiritual knowledge makes a difference—in fact, it makes all the difference in the world.

By reflecting on the first chapter in the Letter of James, readers will bridge the information age today within the formation age of the early church. James provides a pillar, standing as a witness, to restore the world by building a foundation for the future while considering it "nothing but joy" (James 1:2).

This generational bridge is built by spiritual mentors. This is where you, the readers of this book, are needed. As mentors, you will help, not with easy answers or sugarcoating the truth but rather, by walking alongside the younger generation who are living a life much different from ours, but where Christian spiritual knowledge from the church tradition can be trusted and is real.

David Kinnaman and Mark Matlock published *Faith for Exiles* in 2019, and by providing a starting point for spiritual mentors and the next generation of resilient disciples, it promises: "Realism + hope = resilience."[2] Resilience is an important description. It has to do not only with strength but with the ability to rebound and bounce back not ever the same, but with a greater vision and hope for tomorrow. Think pandemic. What I have written is not a training manual nor a stairstep approach for becoming a spiritual mentor. Rather, this is a reflection on the Letter of James that sets a spiritual foundation for lifestyle change in Christ and encourages forging meaningful, intergenerational relationships.

If I contribute, it will be in letting James speak not from a long, long time ago, but to a younger generation today, that experiences mistrust and isolation but seeks authenticity and transparency. In reading James, we find integrity. James spent more time with Jesus than anyone else. James is the real deal. He is authentic. He also encourages spiritual growth by telling us simply and most eloquently to be "be doers of the word" (James 1:22).

My prayer is that after reading this book, you will be

doers. Young adults have plenty of information. What they need is spiritual formation. And what is required is God with flesh, an incarnate faith in Jesus Christ. Parish spiritual mentors have never been as important as they are today. Should you accept the call, this book will be not only worth reading, but doing. Below are five pegs on which we will hang our thoughts from Barna Research in doing the work of mentoring:

1. Train for vocational discipleship
2. Form a resilient identity, experiencing intimacy with Jesus
3. Forge meaningful, intergenerational relationships
4. Develop muscles of cultural discernment
5. Engage in countercultural mission[3]

By merging these insights from Barna into goals, the church strives first for communication, calling upon the church to interact within the kingdom of God. Communion follows by sharing and exchanging kingdom attributes for church life. Community in Christ then replaces social isolation with a witness to bring all generations together as God's will is done on earth, as in heaven.

PART ONE: CHURCH VOCATION—COMMUNICATION

Our first goal recognizes the importance of vocation. Vocation derived from the Latin *vocàre*, which means "to call." A vocation, or calling, is extended to everyone. Our focus will be more specific by helping those who hear the call of Jesus, "the time is fulfilled, and the kingdom of God has come near" (Mark 1:15). By following Jesus, we learn to interact with him in his kingdom. This vocation, or calling, requires discernment. To discern the call is where mentors are needed. Having been formed in Christ, mentors identify the kingdom as a way of living in relationship with Jesus who governs our lives. Mentors know if there is a kingdom, then there is a king. And the king communicates the nature of the kingdom. Following

King Jesus forms our identity and makes for resilient disciples.

PART TWO: CHURCH ATTRIBUTES—COMMUNION

In the first chapter of his letter, James identifies maturity as a characteristic of the church whose identity is in Jesus. Maturity requires the prayer of faith. James further strengthens this claim by showing no partiality. God seeks to send the church where help is most needed. Requiring discernment and navigation, the mentors and the next generation are in communion with a sure and certain hope. By learning to value ourselves in more ways than money, yet to respond with generosity, the community of faith finds security in God from where every perfect gift is given. Here is where the church makes a difference by restoring the world and interacting within the kingdom of God today.

PART THREE: CHURCH WITNESS—COMMUNITY

The first chapter in the Letter of James brings us into a community of ongoing discipleship that further advances the kingdom of God and his righteousness. Listening is held out to the church as a community for all ages to not only hear but do the Word. The importance of nurturing the faith discerns the complexities of our culture by embracing this living word of God now implanted in our very souls. James's firsthand experience of the resurrection leads us in worship of the living Christ—as doers of the word and not hearers only.

PART ONE

THE CHURCH VOCATION: COMMUNICATION

How do we discover our calling? Or how does our calling discover us? We discover it by embarking upon a journey. The journey to get there is a necessary part of the calling itself. Many of us will not know at an early age what our calling is. That does not mean we have no calling. It is already in us, like a bulb lying dormant in the frozen ground, waiting for spring to arrive, so that it can burst through the ground. Our deep sense of calling should send us on a journey of discovery. We have to travel to get where God wants us to go. It is not an easy path we must follow.

—**Jerry Sittser**, *The Will of God as a Way of Life*   [1]

Vocational discipleship means knowing and living God's calling—understanding what we are made to do—especially in the arena of work, and right-sizing our ambitions to God's purposes.

—**David Kinnaman & Mark Matlock**, *Faith for Exiles*   [2]

CHAPTER 1

James—a Living Link to Jesus

In 2001, Oded Golan contacted Andre Lemaire for advice. A meeting followed. From all appearances, the consultation between the two men seemed routine. Golan was a collector of Israeli antiquities and well known as an expert in his field. Based out of the renowned Sorbonne University in Paris, Professor Lemaire was considered one of the finest living epigraphists in the world. An epigraphist is a scientist who studies inscriptions and documents and even scratches and symbols on stones dating back to the earliest of time. From the primeval cultures of long ago to civilizations whose impact remains, an epigraphist interprets and sets in context the strange marks on the material presented and brings it to life and understanding for today.

The meeting would normally be as dry as the bones of the subject discussed, but within no time, newspaper headlines, magazine covers, and television lead stories raced around the world with the tale of an incredible archeological discovery. At the time of the announcement, it sounded like something that took place in the fictional best-selling book by Dan Brown, *The Da Vinci Code*.

But what transpired between the antiquities collector and the renown epigraphist was nonfiction. These two real-life, credible figures presented a story that overnight thrust them upon a stage of intrigue and investigation with jaw-dropping implications. In other words, it was a story about information you can't make up. Or can you?

The initial meeting between Golan and Lemaire revolved around the discovery of the ossuary of James, which soon morphed into an announcement by Hershel Shanks, editor for the *Biblical Archeology Review*, at an October 21, 2002 press conference. Immediately, the story got legs and traveled worldwide. Why would a story about biblical archeology gain such interest? In large part, because the inscription on the ossuary box, a small limestone box that contains the bones of a deceased individual, challenged biblical teaching. For a variety of reasons, the Jews in Israel specifically used this method of burial during the period of the first century BC. In other words, this box was an artifact dated during the time of Jesus. This immediately caught the attention of some.

The inscription on the box revealed the words, "James, son of Joseph, brother of Jesus," and the story then became far more intriguing. This afforded almost overnight proof that Jesus had a brother named James, and Mary had a household of children. The ossuary seemed to potentially hold a different narrative than that of the Bible.

Of course, those familiar with the Bible know about the Letter of James, and throughout Scripture, we find references to brothers and sisters of Jesus. Such an expression can describe a close relationship and not necessarily a biological one. So, did the ossuary really hold a secret or a heresy of some sort, or did it offer important information that could change the scope of church history and present a new direction in church teaching?

Although we can pick on the media for being gullible or biased, this discovery at first had the makings of a true, sensational story. The Israel Antiquities Authority quickly doused the flames of imaginations before academic speculation could become misleading. In 2003, Oded Golan faced forty counts of forgery. The trial lasted seven years with twelve thousand pages of testimony. Agreement of chemical analysis and the study of a microorganism detected on the ossuary concluded the limestone box and the date of the ossuary were genuine. The inscription was considered a forgery. The media dropped the story. And the question of who James is in relation to Jesus remains.

WHO IS JAMES?

In developing our discussion on the Letter of James, the discovery of the ossuary did bring to the surface the question of who James was? Did Jesus have a brother? One glance at the New Testament and Middle Eastern culture finds the name James as common as Mary and Joseph but with some specificity in Scripture. For example, there is James, who is the son of Zebedee, which means he is not the son of Joseph. For the same reason, we rule out the James who is the son of Alphaeus and brother of Matthew, one of the twelve disciples. But interestingly enough, another James is repeatedly identified as "the Lord's brother" (Galatians 1:19), the one most often associated with the Letter of James.

Granted, the idea of Jesus having physical brothers and sisters and a family is nothing new. But it is complicated. The Gospels make repeated references to the family of Jesus. Recall when Jesus came into his hometown and the ensuing crowd cried "Is not his mother called Mary? And are not his brothers James and Joseph and Simon and Judas? And are not all his sisters with us?" (Matthew 13:55). The Gospel of Mark tells a darker story of the same incident where the family of Jesus "restrains" Jesus because the crowd thought "he has gone out of his mind" (Mark 3:22). Furthermore, Joseph is omitted not only in this story but all others as well, creating a long-held presumption that Joseph died soon after the birth of Jesus.

If Joseph died during Jesus's childhood, then we must ask how Mary acquired such a large family? After all, Luke records in his Gospel, Mary "gave birth to her firstborn son and wrapped him in bands of cloth, and laid him in a manger" (Luke 2:7). Jesus was considered firstborn—to the virgin Mary. With respect to sibling order, the early church fathers developed a teaching that Joseph was a widower who brought James and his brothers and sisters from a previous marriage into his relationship with Mary. James has then been traditionally considered a stepbrother to Jesus as Joseph's son. This teaching is further reflected in a second century non-canonical writing attributed to James entitled *The Protevangelium of James*. A mural also found in the crypt of the Benedictine Dormition Abbey in Jerusalem, pictures James holding over his shoulders what might be considered the family possessions, indicating James was a respected authority even at an early age as he walks with Mary, Joseph, and the infant Jesus.

In this mural entitled *The Dream of Joseph and Flight into Egypt,* Joseph dreamed of an angel who warned him to flee to Egypt, because Herod was searching for the child. Jesus is pictured on the shoulder of Joseph. Mary is riding behind with an adolescent or older brother of Jesus, who is identified as Joseph's son, James. Such icons of worship elevated both the family and the role of James as a pillar of the early church. James served as a living link to Jesus by witnessing the resurrection.

JAMES: THE SPIRITUAL MENTOR

As we return to our initial question about the identity of James, we must say proof of the exact relationship between James and Jesus is clouded and difficult to document with pinpoint accuracy. Discovery of the ossuary that supposedly held the bones of James only rekindles wild discussions about James and Jesus, often leading further to speculation and distraction with imaginative stories but contributing little to building the faith. Although the question of identity surfaced, the references to James in Scripture and in early church history portray him as a man who experienced a great change in identity.

From one who reportedly did not believe in Jesus and took great offense at him, James experienced a profound transformation, according to Scripture. Through acts of integrity, one finds identity, and James was a man known for integrity, wisdom, and righteousness. Some traditions hold James, a man of great faith and a pillar of the church, became the first bishop of Jerusalem. In fact, debates rage as to whether he was considered a rival and more of a leader than Peter or Paul. Point being, James was a prominent church figure who focused on Jerusalem and whose ministry clearly brought Jews into the faith of the Messiah Jesus.

Some scholars date the letter James wrote to the church as early as the 40s AD, making it one of the first Christian documents. His message is clear and as straightforward today as then. Because of his identity as a popular leader, and as a result of the persecutions toward the Christians and their worship, James was targeted and viciously martyred. The gruesome details of his death can be found in various accounts of early Christian writings, with the most extensive source written by Eusebius. He tells of James being thrown from the pinnacle of the temple. Though his legs were broken, he was still alive, so they began to stone him, "then struck him on the head by a club and he died."[1]

Death can sometimes provide insight into the life of the person who died and supply an even greater understanding for and deeper appreciation of the legacy left by a loved one. Certainly, the martyrdom of James stands out as a significant event in church history. But rather than define James by his death, we treasure his identity and consequently his life more by his witness to the resurrection. Scripture records the risen Lord "appeared to Cephas, (Peter) then to the Twelve. Then he appeared to more than five hundred brothers and sisters at one time, most of whom are still alive, though some have died. Then he appeared to James, then to all the apostles" (I Corinthians 15: 5–7).

Regardless of all the discussion about who James was, one thing is certain—he became a different person after the resurrection. The early church nicknamed James "camel knees" because his habit of praying for so long caused his knees to become as hard as a camel's. We know this James as one who lived an impeccable life after the resurrection, who wrote a letter to the faith community, and who was one of earliest church spiritual mentors.

WISDOM FROM ON HIGH

According to James, the body of Christ is designed to house the gift of wisdom. Common sense teaches us that wisdom comes from learning by mistakes. Mistakes from the past teach us to avoid repeating those mistakes in the future. Therefore, wisdom is born. For example, if we fall off a bicycle, we theoretically learn wisdom from the proverbial school of hard knocks, and we get up and ride again.

The Letter of James provides an additional understanding of wisdom. James learned not only from his mistakes but from the rich tradition of such writings as Sirach, the Book of Proverbs, and the Book of Job.

Well-grounded in the rabbinical teachings, he satisfied his thirst for wisdom by drinking from the deep well of the Torah and the Law. His prolific understanding further strengthened his spiritual life and character as he tapped into these sources of wisdom. While we can act a little smarter because of learning from our mistakes, wisdom encompasses more than just how we act and react. Rather wisdom is born out of the spiritual understanding of the source of our actions and our character. James writes about this source when he asks "Can a fig tree...yield olives, or a grapevine figs? No more can salt water yield fresh" (James 3:12). When it comes to the church, our source of wisdom resides in our spiritual nature that informs our human nature. The church must always discern and watch out for selfish ambition which corrupts and wreaks havoc upon this source of wisdom from on high, which is another way of referring to something big. Wisdom is big.

The church holds wisdom and must always check envy at the door. James writes the following words of warning to the church regarding selfish ambition and the danger of envy:

> But if you have bitter envy and selfish ambition in your hearts, do not be boastful and false to the truth. Such wisdom does not come down from above, but is earthly, unspiritual, devilish. For where there is envy and selfish ambition, there will also be disorder and wickedness of every kind. (James 3: 14-16)

WISDOM IS STRONGER THAN ENVY

In wondering why James would isolate envy as such a great danger to life in the church, it is apparent envy often makes comparisons or results from a reaction of insecurity or some sort of insufficiency. At a psychological level, we could sit back in our armchairs and question James as to his relationship with his brothers and how he compared to Jesus. Then, we would conclude it is no surprise James seems hung up and obsessed with the problem of envy. In this case, psychology is not the answer. James clearly addresses envy as a profound spiritual problem, and any attempt at a cure requires some sort of spiritual solution or spiritual antidote.

Envy becomes a matter of spirituality when it first and foremost operates in opposition to love. Scripture records, "God is love" (I John 4:8), and if envy is in opposition to love, look out. Before long, envy will go tooth and nail with God. But in the end, envy always loses. The love of God is the strongest force known to man because "it bears all things, believes all things, hopes all things, endures all things. Love never ends" (13 Corinthians 13:7-8).

James wants the church to know there must be no room for envy in the faith community, especially since envy stands against God's love and has the potential of creating disorder on a grand scale with wickedness of every kind. By returning to the source of envy, the church is equipped to offer wisdom as both a necessary resource and a gift to bring healing and assurance to all.

BARNA RESEARCH

Disturbing many Christians is the growing dropout rate of young adults from church membership rolls. In the book *Faith for Exiles*, the research on the perceptions and attitudes show young adults "have access to more knowledge than any other generation in human history." As a result, "Young people are looking to their devices to make sense of the world around them. [But] instantaneous access to information does not equal wisdom."[2] Older generations are amazed by technology, and we pinch ourselves when thinking about the capacity held by an everyday smartphone. With the mere push of a button, we make phone calls around the world, explore bits and pieces of information from search engines, or listen to renown speakers from our favorite podcasts while taking a walk. When our day ends, we order a takeout dinner and plug in our phones so they will be powered up for another day. All this takes place in the palm of a hand.

With growing awareness, we recognize a smartphone cannot effectively move us beyond being consumers of information to people of wisdom. For this next generation, it seems as if a lack of discernment of how to wisely apply knowledge exists in their lives, and the world is limited to the palms of their hands. They appear lost without their handheld phones. And this presents the need for spiritual mentors to bridge the gap between lost and found. It will not be easy, Barna concludes. It will take massive doses of wisdom to make sense and live faithfully in such a rapidly changing culture, yet herein lies the call that reminds the church "God's children in the next generation need more and deserve better."[3] How to measure or quantify "better" is no small task, nor is it a simple matter to identify the "need" of the next generation. What we can do is cast a vision beyond the church walls and see all God's children. This is less about eyesight but more about insight for spiritual mentors who are called and equipped to bridge the gap between the information age and a formation stage. Spiritual mentors then become the adult-in-the-room, who like James, can today communicate a living link to Jesus.

Proverbs teaches "the fear of the Lord is the beginning of wisdom" (Proverbs 9:10). The verse is not designed to scare us. Rather the word "fear" is translated in contemporary versions of Scripture as respect, awe, or reverence of the Lord, implying the holiness of the Lord is the beginning of wisdom. By giving the Lord honor first, we find our priorities shift, our balance and values become clearer, and wisdom from on high reveals itself. Although easy to write, this interior movement is a lifetime process of spiritual growth and transformation when entering the adult world. Not clinging to self-centeredness or putting our own interests first is difficult, but when wisdom abides, envy is less a concern, because with God we are given everything.

James underscores this advice by writing the church "If any of you is lacking in wisdom, ask God" (James 1:5). In other words, stay close to the source of wisdom. It doesn't take much to defeat envy. Little things go a long way. Always remember, Jesus identifies and labels us the "salt of the earth" for a reason. A little bit of salt goes a long way. If *agápē* love is about sacrifice or simply about getting out of the way and putting someone else first, then go ahead, James writes, and "do" it. The church need not smother this next generation with love. A pinch will do. Like salt, God has an ample supply of wisdom and love for the church to rely upon.

James found both wisdom and love revealed in Jesus every day. In fact, an incident at a wedding in Cana of Galilee demonstrated the abundance of God's kingdom where nothing was lacking. It was a sign. Like a spiritual guide, it directed the church toward more to come. God's kingdom spills over with love and wisdom and salt. Like wine, wisdom flows abundantly.

CHAPTER SUMMARY

- James was considered the brother of Jesus (Galatians 1:19). He is a living link to Jesus. His life experience formed a resilient identity in leading the early church and reaching out to the next generation.
- The Letter of James provides one of the earliest examples of the need for wisdom especially in a culture changing rapidly and filled with insecurity. Our spiritual nature informs our human nature as

James writes, "can a fig tree yield olives?" reminding us we are made for a purpose (James 3:12) and wisdom for a deeper understanding of God at work in our lives.

- Envy is an aspect of our spiritual nature that can be transformed by love. By casting a vision beyond the church walls, we are given the vision to reach out to the next generation through spiritual mentors who are called to bridge the information age with the formation stage.

- Spiritual mentors can make a difference by pulling together threads of meaning for those entering adulthood. No longer clinging to self-centeredness, nor putting one's own interest first, mentors seek wisdom and love, so envy is less a concern. With God we are given everything needed.

Following each chapter review is either a suggested resource or an idea and questions designed to help a parish begin structuring a practice for spiritual mentors with the next generation.

A SPIRITUAL EXERCISE: GETTING STARTED

- WARNING: As spiritual mentors, DO NOT go it alone. Start with prayer. Meet with the church staff and outline an agreed upon proposal.

- Identify young adults who may be interested in meeting for a well-defined, short term relationship, that helps the young adults reflect upon and discern a next step in direction for life, career, and faith in Jesus Christ.

- Depending on the number of mentors and mentorees, pair-up and discuss the purposes of the relationship from the outset for both the mentor and the young adult. Be clear about a plan for spiritual mentoring. Make a "Mentoring Covenant." Allow time for questions, goals, expectations, and some sense of desired outcomes.

SAMPLE MENTORING COVENANT[4]

We commit to the following:

The purpose of our meetings is _____

The spiritual goals we want to work on are_____
_____

The personal life goals we want to work on are _____
_____

The focus of our meetings (ex. study, prayer, discussion, spiritual disciplines) is _____
_____

For the young adult:

As a result of these meetings, how do you want to be different? _____

We agree to prioritize these meetings and meet regularly at _____

We agree to commit to meet for _____ weeks together, with a time to reevaluate, enter and exit after that time.

We agree to pray regularly for each other.

We agree to come prepared for our meetings.

We agree to maintain confidentiality regarding prayer requests and personal sharing.

_____   _____
  Young Adult Signature   Mentor Signature

CHAPTER 2

JESUS THE KING

As we continue our reflection on James, we will look at some of the activities recorded in Scripture that specifically reveal further details about the relationship between Jesus and James. We know James walked alongside Jesus, and he knew Jesus longer than any other disciple. Although James did not write a gospel describing his experience, his letter is filled with quotes and parallels that can be found in the Sermon the Mount. James is an eyewitness. That fact should be enough to accept his authority and his writing but more important is his faith in Jesus as the Risen Lord, the Messiah, the King in the Kingdom of God.

Like Jesus, James came out of Nazareth, a small-town fishing village, and was no doubt aware of the insult intended by Nathanael's sarcastic comment, "Can anything good come out of Nazareth?" (John 1:46). The reply to Nathanael by Philip to, "come and see" invites us to go deeper, knowing there is more going on in Nazareth.

Nazareth means "branch" in Hebrew. Isaiah prophesized of Jesus, "A shoot shall come out of the stump of Jesse and a branch shall grow out of his roots. The spirit of the Lord shall rest on him, the spirit of wisdom" (Isaiah 11:1-2). James witnessed and had a first-hand experience with this source of wisdom and holiness as he grew with Jesus from the same branch out of Nazareth.

As James writes his letter to the church, his source is Jesus. Even though James knew Jesus longer than anyone else in Scripture, their relationship was not based on time. Instead, their relationship grew into a belief and faith that Jesus is who he says he is. Belief and faith originate as a gift from God, shaped by truth and learning. The learning is not necessarily an objective learning—that is, not facts and figures or policies and procedures—but comes through the practice of trust. For some of us, the reliability found in faith takes time to acquire, while for others it can cause an immediate change in direction. This acquisition of faith is not so much about how much time—as it is the right time.

For James, there were several times that for whatever reason, did not seem like the right time, and his faith did not open him at such times to a greater vision of trust in Jesus. In the Gospel of John, we find no record, for example, of James's attending the baptism of Jesus and seeing a dove descending from heaven. Nor was James identified in the same company when Andrew told his brother, Peter, "we have found the Messiah" (John 1:41). Again, it was Philip, who reached out to Nathanael, describing Jesus as the fulfillment of Moses and the prophets. At first, Nathaniel saw no way the Son of God could emerge from a place like Nazareth. But as Jesus spoke about knowing Nathanael, his knowledge was not a superficial, stereotypical sort of recognition. Rather Jesus knew Nathanael from the inside out. Jesus knew Nathanael's identity, his inner essence, his value, and his worth as a child of God. At that time, Nathanael by his presence recognized immediately Jesus was the Son of God. James by his absence did not. James is not mentioned.

Chapter two in the Gospel of John tells of the time James attended a wedding in Cana of Galilee with Jesus. Yesterday, as today, what happened at the wedding in

Cana no doubt seems strange and unbelievable to anyone. The wedding comes almost like an interlude in John's gospel until he tells his readers the wedding in Cana is the first sign to reveal the glory and the light that Jesus is "the Messiah, the Son of God, and through believing you may have life in his name" (John 20:31). The fact that James was present does not make the wedding the right time for James to understand the full revelation of Jesus. James simply does not get it. After the celebration, the disciples and the brothers, including James, go with Jesus back to Capernaum. This could be the end of the story. But a wedding says more. A wedding is the beginning. A miracle also says more. For John, the wedding at Cana constituted a sign pointing to the kingdom of God.

THE KINGDOM LACKS NOTHING

The wedding at Cana of Galilee opens with these words: "On the third day there was a wedding" (John 2:1). Naturally, church people immediately open their eyes when we hear a story about Jesus that begins on the "third day." The third day is the day of the resurrection, and it reminds us of Easter, a day of new life, the beginning of a new creation. The church considers Easter a holy day, a day when God acts. The time is right. A wedding is evidence of God's actions, his involvement in our world, and is a sign of God's love entering within the lives of two people. Two people, formerly unknown to one another, have been brought together by God's extraordinary love. They now intimately know one another. Two become one. Sometimes we refer to a particular marriage as made in heaven. Or we might simply call it a miracle. Either way, love comes from on high. Love originates in the kingdom of God.

The story goes on. Mary, the mother of Jesus, tells Jesus "they have no wine" (John 2:3). They have run out at the reception. Such an oversight is a disgrace to all, especially humiliating for the wedding party and the father of the bride. But in this request for help, Jesus reacts to his mother with a puzzling question. "Woman, what concern is that to you and to me? My hour has not yet come" (John 2:4). For some it appears as if Jesus is a little harsh or flippant with his mother, but as we look deeper into his response, we realize Jesus is operating in an alternate time frame, and his power is rooted in a different realm. The kingdom of God is ushered in by Jesus, but the manifestation and our interaction in his kingdom will not be available until the climactic moment of the resurrection. For now, the wedding at Cana provides—as the Gospel of John records—a sign of the time to come.

The Greeks have two words for time: *chrónos* time and *kairós* time. Chronos, from which the word chronological derives, refers to the understanding of time, and as most commonly used, a way of measuring time that quantifies every moment of every day. It is a finite, precise, closed way of referring to time. Another dimension to time, recognized in biblical days, describes God's time, an expectant time, a way of describing not an event in time but a timeless, open, eternal event. This is kairos time. As Jesus looks at his mother, he recognizes she is not on his time. Nor is James. Hence his response "my hour has not yet come" (John 2:4).

Next, Jesus changes water from six nearby stone water jars, used for purification rites, into wine. Immediately everyone comments on the quality of the wine. But don't forget the quantity. Each stone water jar held approximately thirty gallons. When multiplied by six jars, this amounts to 180 gallons or 900 bottles of wine. It is a crazy amount of wine. Filling cups or wineskins would require only a fraction of what they now have available at the reception. This is a sign of the kingdom of God. Where there was once scarcity, there is now abundance. Where there were six jars, symbolically signifying an incomplete number in the week, Jesus provides the source for a seventh jar, completing the week like the fulfillment of the Sabbath. What once seemed ordinary becomes by all counts extraordinary. Jesus is a change agent, who in one swift move transforms humiliation and embarrassment into joy and celebration. And the greater miracle is for the bride and groom, where two people became one flesh—a miracle.

John does not tell this story about Jesus as if he performs a magical act for a bunch of over-served adults who only want more to drink. Mirroring the body of Christ in action, Christ's actions convey the message of the church, that in the kingdom of God "I shall not want." God's kingdom is not about scarcity. It is about abundance. As the psalmist writes, "My cup overflows" (Psalm 23:5).

No doubt, changing water into wine left many shaking their heads. Others probably considered the wedding reception the talk of Galilee, at least for a few days. For the disciples, however, we read a remarkably different interpretation. "Jesus did this, the first of his signs, in Cana of Galilee, and revealed his glory and his disciples believed in him" (John 2:11). Notice it says the disciples believed. It does not say James believed. Like changing water into wine, so the omission of James and his lack of faith, guides us to the development of faith found in James and in the church for today. We do not always find faith overnight. But we can always find faith in Jesus. That is where we begin for James and the church.

A SIGN POINTING TO HOLINESS

Just because the disciples saw the glory of God revealed in Jesus, does not mean everyone had a vision of glory, as James's case demonstrates. We should not indulge in finger-pointing and ridiculing James for his apparent unbelief at Cana as some commentaries are quick to do. If we study the deeper issue of holiness, we avoid thinking of James as a bad brother who had issues with Jesus and his family of origin. Setting aside all the psychological baggage and contemporary armchair diagnosis, look at the wedding in Cana for what it is—a first sign. Reading the Letter of James, we find Jesus intimately bound and literally interrelated with every word and thought James expresses in his letter. James reveals Jesus as does Cana. Both the sign at Cana and the words of James point us in the direction of holiness.

Granted, as soon as we refer to being holy, an avalanche of skeptics will raise their eyebrows and cast all kinds of aspersions on Christians, for acting as if we are, "holier than thou." Strangely, in our contemporary culture, being holy almost has a bad connotation. We rarely see it applied in our everyday vocabulary. In fact, most people are reluctant to use "holy" as a way of describing themselves. We don't discuss it in a job interview or list it on a résumé when identifying our characteristics, skills, or strengths. Perhaps the only thing worse than being considered holier than thou, is the term "hypocritical." And yet, the holiness of James, both in his devotion to God and his leadership in the church, is legendary. Moreover, James wants this same holiness for you and me and the church today.

Consider this as well: if you are uncomfortable with the word holiness, try leading an unholy life. After all, if being holy is so bad and if no one wants to be thought of as holier than thou, then go ahead and be unholy. Give it a shot. See what happens. Granted, such reasoning is naturally a bit facetious, but the point is clear. Being unholy is a destructive way of living.

The word *érgon* in Greek is often translated as something that "works well," or something that is "functional." Since the time of Aristotle, it also applied to holiness or a holy person. A holy person in other words was considered functional. Today we might call an unholy person "dysfunctional." When Christians function or work well in a manner that responds to the way in which

God designed us, we say they live a holy life. An unholy life works against the way God created us, which simply means we are not working with God. When we are working against God, we find ourselves separated from him and caught up in sin. The result of being unholy might be considered a warning sign, or at least point to trouble that is fast approaching.

Holiness provides something of an antidote to sin and self-destruction and delivers a profound reminder, to remain holy and work with God.

Back to the wedding of Cana in Galilee—something very unusual happened. Water turned into wine. One aspect of holiness is to function well, which means we do what needs to be done and when it should be done. Mary told Jesus they had no more wine. Jesus could have walked away. Instead, he responds. Jesus is able to do what needs to be done—and then some. As we push the story a little further, we see the changing of water into wine reflects a supernatural power, one in relationship with the power of God. Jesus is rooted in the supernatural, a greater realm. This realm is the kingdom of God.

We consider the source of Jesus's holiness, and the abundance of wine, and realize Jesus is working in and functioning within the kingdom of God, his source of holiness. Through the climactic event of the resurrection, we now have access to the kingdom of God in Jesus. Jesus ushers in the kingdom of God with the announcement "the time is fulfilled, and the kingdom has come near" (Mark 1:15). It is kairos time, God's time. As a result of the resurrection, we are now capable of living in this time with our source of holiness and the anointed king, Jesus.

Jesus, the King

The fact the kingdom of God exists means there must be a king. Recall during the time of Samuel when the people rejected God as king and called upon Samuel to "give us a king to govern us" (I Samuel 8:6). From then on, the search for a king, a savior, a messiah, the son of God, a new David, Elijah, Moses, someone, anyone who will restore Israel and lead the people into new life tells the long and winding story of our salvation. Many looked to Jesus as such a political king or a military or revolutionary leader who would indeed fulfill the prophecies of old and overthrow "the yoke of their burden, and the bar across their shoulders and the rod of the oppressor" (Isaiah 8:4) and usher a new reign of power that would crush the kingdom of Herod and the harsh rule of Caesar.

Recall the trial of Jesus before the conniving Pilate, the Roman-appointed procurator, who deftly inquires of Jesus, "Are you the King of the Jews?" (John 18:33). Jesus does not avoid the question of power, authority, and leadership but rather provides the eternal answer for all who follow him. He no longer answers Pilate with words but with action. In his death and resurrection, in the dawning of the new creation, his torn robes and crown of thorns, and the empty tomb all respond forever to Pilate's unanswered question with an invitation to, "come, all you that are weary and are carrying heavy burdens, and I will give you rest. Take my yoke upon you and learn from me" (Matthew 11:28). The law and the prophets are fulfilled, and we are no longer separated from a life with God by sin. Instead, an unending life becomes available now with Jesus, the king of the kingdom of God. According to New Testament scholar Scot McKnight, the kingdom of God is still the kingdom of God, "but it is God who has given himself to Jesus."[1]

King Jesus is the source for our understanding here on earth just as it is in heaven of God's rule, and as McKnight concludes, in Jesus we clearly see how "kings determine what their kingdoms are like."[2] Again, and again, we turn to the parables of Jesus and learn about the kingdom of God. When we hear the Sermon on the Mount with "ears to hear" we are "astounded at his teaching for he [teaches us] as one having authority, and not as their scribes" (Matthew 7:29). James and his letter to the church reflects this authority.

Through his relationship with Jesus, James receives the gift of life eternal in the kingdom of God and writes, "Blessed is anyone who endures temptation. Such a one has stood the test and will receive the crown of life that the Lord has promised to those who love him" (James 1:12). Those words are written by a person who is closely linked to Jesus and given a crown by more than a brother. He obtained it from the king of God's kingdom. This understanding of inheriting the kingdom of God is not a result of a bloodline or a genetic privilege but returns us to the source of our faith which we will turn our attention next.

CHAPTER SUMMARY

- The story of the relationship between James and Jesus does not get off to much of a start. The baptism of Jesus, the encounter with Nathaniel and Phillip, the wedding at Cana, all provide insight into the revelation of Jesus as the Son of God. The time is not right for James.
- *Kairos* time is God's time, a time and life experience when God is revealed. The sign of changing water into wine, is a reminder Jesus is a change agent who transforms life by ushering in the kingdom of God.
- In the kingdom there is a king, a ruler, a lord, one who accepts authority and responsibility for life in the kingdom. Through the sign of changing water into wine we experience the abundance of life in the kingdom and the priority on holiness. The king reflects the kingdom and holiness abounds.

A Spiritual Exercise:

A Rule of Life

The first task as spiritual mentor is that of helping your young adults develop a "rule." The understanding a rule goes back to the early monastic life, and it should be undertaken not as a pain but as a gift to develop and grow the spiritual and community life for all involved. Here is an example of how your mentee might develop a rule:

• Start where you are—and not where you are not.

Silence: if you are bothered by noise, honking horns, constant chatter, nonstop music—you name it—start your "rule" with silence. Think of silence as golden. Use quiet time to slow down. Perhaps use a verse as a mantra: "The Lord is my shepherd (breathe in) I shall not want (breathe out).

Solitude: if your day or life is always busy and is in perpetual motion, "Be still and know that God is God" (Psalm 46:10). Be at peace. Rid yourself of stress, anxiety and worry. "Hurry is not of the devil. Hurry is the devil."

Reflect: Picture your day. (If you do this when you wake up, picture yesterday. If you do this at night before bed, recall hour-by-hour your day and reflect upon each hour, the people, conversations, experiences, etc.)

Review: Looking over your day, identify blessings and where God was present. Feel free to examine curses and where God might have been absent. No need to evaluate. Simply catch hold of the spirit within your day.

Take my yoke: Turn your day over to the Lord. It is a day that will never be repeated. Consider the day a gift—good or bad. Yoke yourself to Christ. Take a moment to think what you and the Lord might do together tomorrow.

- **Prayer:** Should you have a prayer life established, write it out and share it together. Some use the acronym **A-C-T-S,** and pray first in adoration (I adore you Lord for...), then confession (I regret this occurring...), followed by thanksgiving (especially for blessings...) that may have caught your attention, and finally supplication (specific requests or petitions), which opens us to prayer and reliance upon God.
- **Journal:** if you would find it helpful during this period of prayer and time of direction write down insights, thoughts, happenings, and a sentence or two where you find yourself, emotionally, spiritually, relationally.
- **Enjoy!** Fill in the blank.

- **Communication** After a rule has been established, the mentor and the mentees should have a common ground in discussing the place of prayer in their spiritual lives. What have they learned? Has Jesus helped, nudged, or appeared in some way, shape, or form? If so, how? If not, why not? Discuss the efficacy of prayer. Communication is necessary for a relationship to thrive. Prayer is one way to communicate.

CHAPTER 3

CALLING THE CHURCH INTO THE KINGDOM

Late one night, Nicodemus, a leader of the Pharisees, came to visit Jesus. Whether or not the meeting was a clandestine encounter or simply a private appointment, the word obviously got out, and the Gospel of John now records the encounter for all ages. We listen in on this intense conversation with their back-and-forth exchange, including Jesus's saying, "No one can enter the kingdom of God without being born of water and Spirit" (John 3:5). Nicodemus appears clueless, and he apparently walks away back into the darkness, dazed, and hearing only the final words of Jesus: "those who do what is true come to the light" (John 3:21).

Entering the kingdom of God is where we experience life with God. We need not wait until we die to find this life. It is a life available now by understanding that for a kingdom to exist, it requires a king. Further, a king reveals something about his realm.[1] The kingdom reflects his characteristics and personality, and only he grants permission to enter. Entrance is not simply a feeling, or a hunch, or even a matter of the heart. It begins with a calling that requires a transformation and a desire to do God's will on earth as it is in heaven. Jesus grants permission to enter the kingdom, and we find the way through water and the power of the Holy Spirit.

This symbolism may seem foreign to those who have not served under such a reign, but we want to focus on how Jesus refers to the kingdom of God and the requirement of being born by water and spirit. Being born obviously means a new life, a new creation, and a new identity. It is a life designed with the purpose to restore creation to its original purposes. Entering the kingdom of God requires then a different understanding of life. God rules in Jesus, and the Spirit is ever present in this new life. Notice the Spirit is the source of our birth. We are first and foremost spiritual beings. Jesus refers to the Spirit as being like wind or like air that moves within and without and surrounds us. It can't be missed. It is present. Like air, it is invisible but still real. Wind and air are natural elements for life. By breathing in the Spirit, just like we breathe in air, we suck in the very life of God, who in turn brings our spiritual being into existence. But there is more.

Jesus tells Nicodemus that to enter the kingdom, we must be born with water. So often, we think Jesus is referring to baptism. Water cleanses, to be sure, and washes away sin. It also symbolizes the waters breaking and spilling out of the mother at birth. The image is descriptive, but we can go deeper. When Jesus refers to water as a necessary element required to enter the kingdom, think for a moment where we would be without water. Our existence and our very survival depend upon it. It hydrates our bodies so all our organs, cells, and tissues function properly. Keep working with this image of water and picture a fish. Recall the expression, "if you want to know what water is, don't ask the fish." A fish has never lived outside of water. A fish has no way of describing water because that environment is all the fish knows. We can understand and describe it because we look at it from a different perspective. So, Jesus is saying as we enter the kingdom of God through our new life in Christ, we will know the spirit that keeps us alive and afloat. No longer are we human beings trying to understand the spiritual life, but rather we are now spiritual beings who are figuring out what it means to be a human being.

THE BROTHERS AND JESUS

We enter the kingdom of God through a process of transformation. Transformation means change. It also means growth. Unfortunately, some only want to grow and have nothing to do with change. Spiritual transformation requires both change and growth in Christ.

James appears again in chapter seven of John's gospel. At first, the words read like an awkward exchange between Jesus and his brothers and sound as if the brothers are teasing or taunting Jesus. Scholars and commentators take it one step further. They look at the sibling discussion more seriously and consider it unbelief, depicting the brothers, including James, in a bad light for such bantering with Jesus. Here is what the brothers say as the Jewish Festival of Booths (Sukkot) approaches,

> Leave here and go to Judea so that your disciples also may see the works you are doing; for no one who wants to be widely known acts in secret. If you do these things, show yourselves to the world. (For not even his brothers believed in him). (John 7:3-5)

By exploring the brothers' comments further, three important movements come to the surface, impacting a deeper understanding of spiritual transformation and more importantly, the invitation Jesus extends to enter the kingdom of God.

FROM A BOOTH TO THE KINGDOM

The first movement appears to be a geographical one. The brothers request Jesus leave Galilee and go to Judea where he can participate in the Festival of Booths like every other man. This sacred celebration was one of three appointed festivals males were required to observe in Jerusalem. The weeklong observance recalled the temporary booths or shelters used by the Jews while on their forty-year wilderness journey.

At the festival, participants thank God for the daily manna or bread and for sustaining their ancestors lives with the water God provided while in the desert. Whether sincere or not, the brothers encourage Jesus, the so-called messiah, to attend the festival and, by all means, to obey the law. What James and the others are telling Jesus seems to be obvious—obey the law, do what everybody else is doing, worship as they say, and try to fit in. Look the part. Show yourself. See and be seen. The mighty acts of God are always remembered by the righteous ones, especially those attending the festival. By celebrating these acts from the past, the brothers imply Jesus could at least act righteous as well. James would soon learn external acts of righteousness alone do not always reflect the character of the person within.

Recall the Sermon on the Mount when Jesus profoundly and unequivocally says, "Unless your righteousness exceeds that of the scribes and Pharisees you will never enter the kingdom of heaven" (Matthew 5:20). At first blush, our reaction may be such righteousness of the scribes and Pharisees is impossible to attain. Jesus has set the bar too high. We question how anyone can top the Pharisees when it comes to righteousness. If the Pharisees cannot enter the kingdom, then those of us who are not exactly righteous don't stand a snowball's chance … where it gets hot.

Of course, Jesus is speaking directly to sin and the corruption of human character. The bar is not high. We can exceed the scribes and Pharisees' righteousness. On the outside, Jesus points out, the Pharisees look good, but their interior lives are as unrighteous as can be. Jesus wants us to be good people. By that, Jesus means he wants us as good on the inside as we are on the outside.

He wants our words integrated with our behavior, so a cloak of integrity wraps us. Righteousness is not about an external, compulsory act, ritual, or lip service, which only gives thanks to a distant God from long, long time ago. Rather, Jesus "takes delight in the law" like trees growing and "planted by streams of water, which yield their fruit in its season" (Psalm 1:3). Goodness and righteousness are natural, and our thoughts and words with our deeds and action grow like ripe fruit.

At first, Jesus was reluctant to go to Judea because some were looking for an opportunity to kill him. Having delivered the Sermon on the Mount, he clearly separated himself from false righteousness as found in the Pharisees. As a result, he made enemies when he told his listeners they could exceed the righteousness of the Pharisees, and his listeners—not the Pharisees—could enter the kingdom of God. Obviously, these were divisive fighting words to the Pharisees. An encouragement given toward women and children and the sick and poor, along with a mountainside of sinners, sounded like blasphemy. This talk of Jesus—heard in the Sermon on the Mount—was reason enough for death by stoning.

With this, Jesus turns our attention to murder. Although murder is against the law, the Pharisees found sins in the Torah that were loopholes and punishable by death—for example, children cursing their parents could be put to death. Jesus speaks to the source of murder—anger. He makes the point that anger does not exist in the kingdom of God, much less murder. If we want to enter the Kingdom, we leave anger behind.

Jesus then follows with a reference to adultery. The Pharisees know adultery is against the law, and it too carries a penalty of death by stoning. True, adultery is a violation of faith and commitment resulting in sin, but Jesus calls on us to look within and examine lust. The seeds of adultery grow from lust. In one swift move,

Jesus reveals the Pharisees are filled with not only anger but lust as well. Once again, lust does not exist in the kingdom of God nor does adultery. Apparent is that though the Pharisee appears righteous on the outside, in order to enter the kingdom of God, they need to cleanse themselves on the inside of anger and lust.

Now, the kingdom of God is not just about leaving behind anger, murder, or adultery. Our job, through the process of transformation, is to invite the Holy Spirit within and spiritually wash ourselves of all that corrupts the heart, mind, and soul of anger and lust and the forces that separate us from the love of God. James is one of the first to hear these words and warnings with "ears that hear."

He also hears the promises and the possibilities found in exceeding the righteousness of the Pharisees and entering the kingdom of God. Years later in his letter, this integrity between the interior and the exterior of life becomes paramount in both his witness and his writing as he professes, "For just as the body without the spirit is dead, so faith without works is also dead" (James 2:26).

James learns his lesson about righteousness and about entering the kingdom, and he brings this gift home to the church. Jesus holds out the promise of entering the kingdom by not burdening us with more rules to live by. Rather God enters our lives by the Holy Spirit. Here, he cleanses us in ways the law fails to observe. With water, Jesus redeems and heals the interior life, so we may learn to live with God—not in a tent, but in the kingdom of God. The Pharisees never grasped this spirit nor drank from these waters of redemption. But for those who seek entrance into the kingdom of God, the Spirit and water direct the way.

From Unbelief to Belief

In the exchange between Jesus and the brothers, a second remark further impacts our spiritual life and directs our attention to entering the kingdom of God. James and his brothers tell Jesus they want the disciples to "see the works" and they encourage Jesus to "show" himself to the world. As with the request of going to Judea simply to obey the law, this idea of attending the festival so the disciples may see the works of Jesus is problematic. As Jesus said to his mother at Cana, so he says to his brothers, "my time has not yet come" (John 7:6). Jesus is not on the same timeline with his brothers.

He tells his brothers they will always live in this chronos time, but Jesus lives in eternal, kairos time—that is, God's time. The kairos reality Jesus describes is being revealed through ushering in the kingdom of God that will break through time and space and memory. Furthermore, Jesus is no entertainer or vaudeville act. Much like the changing of water into wine at the wedding at Cana, Jesus's miracles demonstrate he cares deeply about his ability to literally shepherd in the works and presence of God. For now, he anticipates God doing a great work within his disciples. Recall Jesus saying to them, "the one who believes in me will also do the works I do, in fact, will do greater works than these" (John 14:12). Immediately after saying this, Jesus then promises his disciples the gift of the Holy Spirit.

The Holy Spirit, like water, penetrates us within by reinforcing our relationship with Jesus and by bringing about the transformation in our lives, so we are equipped to do what needs to be done. Recall when Jesus met with Nicodemus and emphasized the spirit as a necessary requirement for entering the kingdom. He says this because everyone is spiritual and because all kinds of spirits exist—some are good and some are evil. We need to be careful as we discern this spiritual world, but Jesus assures us the Spirit he gives is holy. The Holy Spirit makes us whole by relating and uniting us to the will of God, so what God wants done is done here on earth just as it is in heaven. After all, that is what we ask in the Lord's prayer. The answer to this petition is found through the mighty work of the Holy Spirit as we grasp hold of our faith in Christ and live in the spirit of righteousness.

The Holy Spirit provides us with a spiritual life that has meaning and definition. Granted, the world of the Holy Spirit does not consist of something we can see or touch, but this doesn't make it any less real. The Holy Spirit shapes reality by leading us beyond our mortal and limited finite existence into an eternal destiny found in the kingdom of God. Through attention to the Holy Spirit, we discover gifts that bear fruit and enable us to perform works here on earth. This further provides us with more than eyesight. We develop insight and vision into the heavens where "we see in a mirror, dimly" (I Corinthians 13:12).

Jesus reveals his concern over religious deception in the brief but profound exchange with his brothers. He is troubled by the Pharisees and their hypocrisy and the fact that, although they look good on the outside, their inner life is filthy. As a result, they lead by deception. The brothers almost seem to be no different, as if they are setting a trap much like Joseph's brothers set for their dreamy-eyed sibling. Their admission they do not believe in Jesus only furthers the sense of trickery. Their unbelief can only be changed and transformed by the convicting work of the Holy Spirit at the resurrection and the fullness of kairos time. Only though water and the Holy Spirit will their eyes be washed and cleansed thoroughly to see the kingdom of God and the mighty acts of God at work through the church, the body of Christ. And Jesus will show himself to the world, not in secret but with shouts from the rooftops.

James is one of the first to profess an Easter faith, and we read his admonition to the church, "If any think they are religious, and do not bridle their tongues but deceive their hearts, their religion is worthless" (James 1:26). This movement from unbelief to belief and from deception into truth, provides the faithful with further guidance for entering the kingdom of God.

FROM DRY TO WET

As we listen carefully to the conversation between Jesus and his brothers, the third movement surfaces around the purpose of water. Although the gospel of John does not specifically mention water in these few verses, we see its nuanced presence. Water literally drips throughout his gospel and provides an important passageway into the kingdom of God.

The brothers implore Jesus to participate in the Festival of Booths, where the officiating priest would draw water from the pool of Siloam. Such an act is a reminder of when God provided water after the people had quarreled with Moses, crying out: "Give us water to drink. Why did you bring us out of Egypt, to kill us and our children and livestock with thirst?" (Exodus 17:2-3). After hearing their cry of desperation and quarrel, Moses appealed to God, who sent him to stand on the rock at Horeb. Not precisely following God's instruction, Moses instead struck a rock where water gushed out, and the people drank their fill. He named the place Massah and Meribah meaning a rock of test and quarrel. And as a result of not obeying fully, Moses was not allowed to enter the Promised Land.

Water gives life. The shepherd in the twenty-third psalm leads us "beside still waters" (Psalm 23:2), and Jesus, the shepherd of our souls, guides us to the "springs of the water of life" (Revelation 7:17). From Genesis, the God of creation is described at work using water—shaping and forming the earth, the heavens, the rains, clouds, the seas, and the dry land. The prophecy of Isaiah anticipates the day when "the earth will be full of knowledge of the Lord as the waters cover the sea" (Isaiah 11:9). And at the Festival of Booths, the priest will draw water from the pool of Siloam.

Siloam means "sent." God sent Jesus. He encounters the woman of Samaria at a well, and he asks for a drink. The well can represent going down into the darkness and the unknown. With the Samaritan woman who had five husbands, Jesus uses water and the well, and he goes deep into the mystery of her life. Shortly after drinking from the well with her, we watch Jesus walk on water. Again, it is not a trick, but rather he hears the cry of Peter and all who are sinking, "Lord, save me!" (Matthew 14:30).

As the priest draws water from the pool Jesus heals a man born blind by sending him to that same pool. As the waters rush over the man's eyes, he sees like never before. On the last day of the festival, Jesus cries out, "Let anyone who is thirsty come to me, and let the one who believes in me drink" (John 7:38).

Immediately afterward, Nicodemus—the one who had gone to Jesus at night—appears on the scene and says to the Pharisees "our law does not judge people without first giving them a hearing to find out what they are doing, does it?" (John 7:51) Nicodemus knows there is something in the water. Or perhaps like the Spirit, it is blowing in the wind.

CHAPTER SUMMARY

- Jesus calls the church into kingdom life through the Holy Spirit and water. The kingdom offers life with God and a new creation waiting to be restored. The Pharisees look good outwardly but inwardly are ruined, and the Festival of the Booths becomes a way for Jesus to demonstrate life is not found on more rules and laws to live by, but by water and the Spirit.

- We are in essence spiritual beings from birth who are trying to figure out what in the world our existence means to be a human being. James and his brothers provide further insight when Jesus says to them "My time has not come" indicating both the cross and the importance of finding the right time in transitioning from unbelief to belief. Examples of Moses at Massah and Meribah, and the priest at the pool of Siloam and the announcement of Jesus saying whoever thirst may come to him, are signs that demonstrate the availability of new life that awaits us.
- Life in Christ in water and spirit is where we are transformed by holiness and righteousness. Holiness simply means we function appropriately within as compared to Pharisees who neglected the inner life and as a result could be considered dysfunctional. Righteous describes a good person whose actions come from the character within, rather than an external requirement.
- Nicodemus who first came to Jesus at night (John 3) and listened to the teaching about the kingdom and the necessity of being clean on the inside through water and the Spirit appears again. He asks, "Our law does not judge people without first giving them a hearing to find out what they are doing, does it?" (John 7:51) Clearly, the Spirit and water were working within Nicodemus, and the time was right for his question.

A SPIRITUAL EXERCISE:

Restoration

- As the formation of resilient disciples continues, now might be the time to discuss vocation and restoration or the way of holiness and righteousness.
- Start with a reading and rereading of the Genesis creation story.

- God saw the light and it was good (Gen. 1:3).
- God called the dry lands Earth and the waters Sea. It was good (Gen. 1: 10).
- The earth brought forth vegetation and God saw that it was good (Gen. 1:12)
- God separated the light from darkness and saw that it was good (Gen. 1:18).
- God created animals of every kind and saw that it was good (Gen. 1: 25).
- God made male and female in the image of God. And everything God made was good (Gen. 1:31).
- Take some time and review the story of creation and our life with God. Discuss all that is good about creation. Are there areas of creation that have gone bad? What are you willing to do in restoring creation?
- We are made in the image of God. We do not look like God. We do have attributes of God that can be put into action through stewardship. Choose an area you are interested in restoring.

Creation

Choice (choose life)
Rest(sabbath)
Environment
Activity
Trust
Interpersonal relationships
Outlook
Nutrition[2]

CHAPTER 4

THE CHURCH PARTICIPATES IN THE KINGDOM

The idea of a church is not simply a child's finger-play of "here is the church and here is the steeple." The church *is* the people, the people who sit on the side of a hill and are riveted by the Sermon on the Mount. These same people listen to the parables about the kingdom of God, and they see miracles and signs of God's presence and glory with their own eyes. God demonstrates before them his mission to usher in a kingdom ruled through his son, Jesus, the "King of kings and Lord of lords" (Revelation 19:16).

In Jesus, God makes his creation new, and the people witness this in the paradox of the crucifixion. There at the cross, the veil in the temple is torn open, and the spirit is poured out. No longer do we go to the temple, but the temple now comes to us. As a result of the resurrection, we are the body of Christ, the new creation, formed by the Holy Spirit. The church participates as the feet, hands, and heart of Christ by partaking in the worship, the liturgy, literally "the work of the people" (Gk. *laós érgon,*). The breaking of bread makes the presence of Christ known, and the church is the only organization, institution, or community that breathes in and lives out the kingdom of God as the people of God.

No political system, no business, no technology company, no entertainment speaks for our life in the kingdom of God. Only the church speaks for and participates in the kingdom of God. Of course, people want justice today. But for the church, justice is based on God and in God's judgment. In other words, no kingdom, no justice. Today, people cry out for peace. But again, the peace of God is just that—the peace *of* God—and this peace is based on faith that passes all understanding because peace originates in God's kingdom. Jesus makes us aware if there is no kingdom, there is no peace.

So, the cry continues. People yearn for hope, but our sure and certain hope is unseen. This does not mean hope is unreal because we cannot see it, but it does mean hope is first and foremost spiritual, which once again places hope within the realm of the kingdom of God. Love, agàpē love, does not simply rely on our emotions. Agàpē love is a self-giving, sacrificial, sacred love, located in the kingdom of God where it originates with God, "who first loved us" (I John 4:19). All these attributes and more are made manifest in the kingdom of God by participation in the church. This character is unleashed today, right now.

This engagement and interaction are not new nor necessarily some kind of strategic plan for the church. The kingdom of God does, however, reinforce both the revelation and the incarnation of Jesus as the Son of God. God has turned over the rule of his kingdom to his Son. And James is one of the earliest Christian writers who knows seeking the kingdom of God first begins by following Jesus. His experience of the resurrection transforms him into "a servant of God and the Lord Jesus Christ" (James 1:1). James writes his letter earlier than any of the gospels, and he predates most of Paul's more developed theology. The parallels of this early church document—the witness of James, the mission of the church—is reflected clearly in the later gospels of John and Matthew. The Letter of James seems to indicate a strong tradition in the early church that encourages life in the kingdom—now.

THE LETTER OF JAMES AND THE GOSPEL OF JOHN

James grew up with Jesus. He was a contemporary of Jesus and observed his acts and listened to much of what Jesus said during his earthly ministry. With this eyewitness and first-hand account of Jesus, James fills his letter with sayings and phrases circulated by the word, by the experiences, and as importantly, reinforced by the worship found in early church gatherings. For example, when Jesus says, "seek first the kingdom of God and his righteousness" (Matthew 6:33), no doubt this becomes a message that is circulated and memorized and lived out by all who gather in the fellowship and worship of Jesus. This imperative "to seek first the kingdom" could also have been the mission statement of the early church or simply a common exchange among the faithful. But this priority and mission imperative also includes a strong ethical command that, by seeking the kingdom of God, a life of righteousness is required.

James adopts this understanding of righteousness, as confirmed by the label of "James the Just" or "James the Righteous" given him by the early church. Behind this understanding of righteousness lies a Christlike character, a conversion experience of dying to an old self and rising to the new self in Christ. As mentioned before, some scholars and writers dismiss James and his brothers and sisters as simply opposing Jesus. In the few stories relating to James as written in the Gospel of John, there seems to be a deeper appreciation or sense of spiritually growing in Christ, especially as pertains to the witness of James.

John presents himself in his gospel as the "beloved" disciple and becomes the focal point for the future of the church repository of faith as seen in the crucifixion. The depth of this handoff and the commission Jesus gives to John is captured by John's gospel in a most excruciating yet loving way, as follows:

> Meanwhile standing near the cross of Jesus were his mother, and his mother's sister, Mary the wife of Clopas,

and Mary Magdalene. When Jesus saw his mother and the disciple whom he loved standing beside her, he said to his mother, "Woman, here is your son." Then he said to the disciple, "here is your mother." And from that hour the disciple took her into his own home. (John 19: 25-27).

Although little is written of the relationship between James and John from this point forward, apparently James was influenced by the home of John and by John's continued witness of the Word. The prologue in John's gospel speaks of the new creation Jesus ushers in, and the opening phrase "in the beginning" echoes the Genesis story heard from long ago. Along with the story of Adam and Eve and the first creation, we become well aware of sin and our separation from the will of God. In John's gospel, we read of redemption from sin and salvation that comes to us through Jesus, the incarnate "Word [who] became flesh and lived among us" (John 1:14). Here we find a blend of Greek philosophy and early Christian theology around this understanding of the Word, or in the Greek, the *logos*. *Logos* literally means logic—a logical understanding, a controlling principle, the agent of creation and creativity through which the mystery of God is disclosed to the world. God is revealed by the Word, and this revelation is understood by faith, which becomes the Christian rationale or *raison d'être* for living with God. In Christ, we understand, and we know God in Jesus, who is the word made flesh and who communicates God's word to us. "The word of God for the people of God" is the common liturgical church expression that communicates this deep wisdom found within the early oral tradition of the church.

To take this understanding one step further, we find an additional word that is key to our life of holiness or righteousness. The word is "reckoning," or in the Greek *logizomai,* a word derived from logos. It means that, as a result of our faith in Jesus, we are literally being "worded" into righteousness by Jesus or reckoned as whole and righteous by the Word made flesh.[1] It is important to watch this word reckon or *logizomai* because it imputes an understanding for James and evolves into an understanding for the church to participate in the kingdom now, by being, "doers of the word" (James 1:22).

The Letter of James, and the Gospel of Matthew

Although the Letter of James predates John or Matthew, James apparently was familiar with the sayings of Jesus before the gospels appeared in writing. In reading James, one finds remarkable similarities with Matthew's gospel, especially in the Sermon on the Mount. (See Matthew 5-7)

Even though the Letter of James and Matthew's sayings in the Sermon on the Mount were written years apart, the similarities speak to a common desire of building the early church together. Matthew was known for first being a tax collector and reviled by many because of his profession. Bu Matthew hears the call to "follow me." And he does.

Matthew's gospel further reflects his transformation through an eternal life made available with God in a church that follows Jesus, the new Moses, into a promised land. This land does not consist of boundaries and geography and limitations but a land in the kingdom of God, ruled by the Lord Jesus where each of us is called to now "let our light so shine before men; that they may see your good works, and glorify your Father who is in heaven" (Matthew 5: 16)

Whether or not James was a source for John and Matthew, the early witness of James led the church to be doers of the Word by seeking the kingdom of God and his righteousness by "purifying your hearts" (James 4:8). As Matthew records the Beatitude of Jesus, "Blessed are the pure in heart" (Matthew 5:8). In other words, clearly Matthew and James were on the same page.

THE LETTER OF JAMES

Although our attention will primarily center on the opening chapter in the Letter of James (1:1-27) we'll find that, throughout the letter, James "has a greater frequency of using imperatives more than any other New Testament book."[2] Several of these imperatives appear as chapter headings in this book, but we address it at this point, because James writes a letter for the church today. James does not scold the church. His imperatives are not critical or threatening toward the faithful, since he intends this as a pastoral letter. For example, to those gathered in worship, he uses a gentle touch that is often repeated, "my dear brothers and sisters." The letter is not harsh but encouraging and inspiring especially for the witness of the body of Christ. It provides for us today generational or paternal advice. James could be considered as one of the church's first spiritual mentors.

Be assured however, the condemnation comes and the fire burns when James turns his attention to the culture. Here he implores Christians to participate in the kingdom by being "mature and complete, lacking in nothing" (James 1:4) with the distinct implication that life without Christ leaves us immature, incomplete, and deformed— lacking significance and meaning in life. James does not judge the church, but he also does not hold back when it comes to his disdain for the culture. The letter to the faithful encourages them to strive for a life with God that is promised to the righteous ones who love the Lord and will receive a crown worn in the kingdom. It also provides fair warning that without faith in Christ, a life without righteousness will be no different from the culture or a ship on "the wave of the sea, driven and tossed by the wind" (James 1:7).

With such captivating metaphors and striking imperatives, James instructs the church to move forward through participation in the kingdom of God and his righteousness. We will hear from James over and over that we can best participate by being "doers of the word." But Jesus tells us to seek first God's kingdom and his righteousness. Seeking God's righteousness is really the clue—or better yet, the key—James stresses for us as entrance into the kingdom. Without righteousness, the church is hypocritical.

BEWARE

Two news stories, actually scandals, appeared on the television and social media, momentarily exciting and catching the attention of a weary culture. First, a well-known president of an evangelical university and his wife had engaged in a sordid "Fatal Attraction" type arrangement that went on for several years. The media didn't spare any details and the university took immediate action to remove the president. The story disappeared from the 24/7 news cycle as the media has moved on. But left behind were the students, the faculty, the alumni, and all who supported and respected the college. The broken trust, the scars, and perhaps the loss of faith will linger for years in the wake of unrighteous behavior.

The second example is not far removed. A popular televangelist divorced his wife and, in the settlement, revealed his net worth of over $100 million, including extravagant homes and a Ferrari sports car valued at $4.5 million. Sure, some might excuse the wealth with the comparison that he is not a billionaire, but most Christians lament an abuse of trust and a style of abhorrent leadership.

Both examples reveal an obvious ethical concern and violate biblical standards with respect to our care for the poor and our understanding of being made in the image of God. Specifically, as we reflect on the introduction of the Letter of James, we read his admonition of the rich being brought low, because they "will disappear like a flower in the field" (James 1:10). The same message holds true for a church that loses focuses and relies on the treasures of this world or ignores the Law, bearing false witness against their neighbor.

Poor Christian stewardship and unrighteous conduct speaks directly to "what an ironic tragedy that an affluent, 'Christian' minority in the world continues to hoard its wealth while hundreds of millions of people hover on the edge of starvation!"[3] The world sees such a tragedy on the deception of the unrighteous "Christian" university president and the multi-millionaire televangelist because the smear on the church leaves us all ashamed and feeling the tinge of guilt. Think of the untold number of believers or simply observers of the Christian faith who are hurt by scandals and as a result, turn their backs and walk away from the church never to return.

On a smaller scale, or perhaps a more personal one, think of parents who act one way at church and then act in an entirely different manner at home. Such duplicity may be excused or dismissed time and time again because it seems minimal compared to the greater atrocities in the news, but words matter and so too does our behavior. Our children are watching us. This includes both faith and work. It involves both seeking the kingdom of God and his righteousness.

As we turn to the introduction in the Letter of James, be assured James is writing to a church he loves but also to a church that is fragile. Immoral behavior, misunderstandings, and conflict can all stunt spiritual growth and ultimately render the church witness ineffective and incompetent.

THE BARNA GROUP

The research of the Barna Group has carefully and strategically tracked the role of faith in America for more than thirty years. As a result, they hold a mirror up especially for the church to see the demographics and what the research indicates about the spiritual life of our church and culture. We'll use several of their studies throughout our look at James, but the timeliness and relevance of James speaks to a growing concern expressed by Barna—that is, how young people experience Christianity. The one word that comes across with the greatest frequency in Barna's research is the term "hypocritical." Sadly, today's young people attach the term to the church and, of those who have had sufficient exposure to Christians and churches, they conclude present-day Christianity is hypocritical.[4]

Following the resurrection, the church finds in James a leader who is consistent and trustworthy and who demonstrates an integrity of character so faultless they refer to him as "James the Righteous." We know what it is like to be self-righteous, a label much like "hypocrisy" that no one wants. And yet the opposite of self-righteousness is rarely used. Herein lies the problem. Righteousness and righteous behavior have fallen out of favor at a time when they are perhaps needed most. We seem to have forgotten the teaching Jesus provides on the dangers of wealth and reputation much less seeking the kingdom of God and his righteousness.

In the Letter of James, and later in the Gospels of Matthew and John, we learn to rely on God through transformation of character by participating in kingdom living. James calls this participation "doing the word," and it will make a difference for the church. In fact, it will make all the difference in this world and the world to come. It is to these attributes we now give our full consideration.

CHAPTER SUMMARY

- The church participates in the kingdom of God. This is where God reigns and governs our life through the rule of Jesus, the King of kings. As the body of Christ, we recognize in our worship the presence of Jesus and become the hands and feet of the living Lord.

- The church lives for righteousness by seeking "first for the kingdom of God and his righteousness" (Matthew 6:33) so we may live God's will. James refers to this as "doing the word." The word (*logos*) is a logical understanding through which the mystery of God is disclosed to the world. God is revealed by the Word in the flesh and incarnation of Jesus Christ.

- How to practice and live the word is a matter of righteousness that reflects the image of God daily. To live an unrighteous life hurts the church, and examples abound. Transformation occurs we are under the rule of Christ.

- Following the resurrection, the church finds in James a leader who is consistent, trustworthy and who demonstrates an integrity of character that is faultless. He is referred to as "James the righteous."

Vocational Discipleship

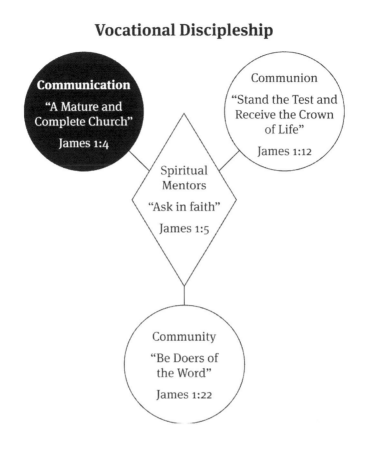

According to Barna Research, "the most heartbreaking aspect of our findings is the utter lack of clarity that many young people have regarding what God is asking them to do in their lives. It is a modern tragedy. This next generation of Christians have no idea that their faith connects to life's work."[5]

- As you read this quote consider being a mentor to the next generation. Be willing to sit down and communicate with a young adult. Based on "Part One" of your reading reflect on your vision for a life of meaning, purpose and direction for yourself and this next generation. Be doers of the word.

PART TWO

THE CHURCH ATTRIBUTES: COMMUNION

The church is only the church to the degree that it lives under King Jesus. We call Jesus "Lord," and that means he is our Lord and we are the Lord's servants as kingdom citizens. We are not "under the Lord" when we do our part as Christians—at home, in the church—but then "under Caesar" when acting as public citizens. If Jesus is Lord, he is always Lord—at home, in the church, and in the public. We don't have an ethic for our Christian life and another ethic for our public, worldly, secular life. We have one ethic because Jesus is Lord overall.

—Scot McKnight, *Kingdom Conspiracy* [1]

Resilient Disciples are "Christ followers who (1) attend church at least monthly and engage with their church more than just attending worship services; (2) trust firmly in the authority of the Bible; (3) are committed to Jesus personally and affirm he was crucified and raised from the dead to conquer sin and death; and (4) express desire to transform the broader society as an outcome of their faith.

—David Kinnaman & Mark Matlock, Faith for Exiles[2]

CHAPTER 5

THE CALL

"LACKING IN NOTHING"

(JAMES 1:4)

When I was a young adult, I joined the Beatles in singing "All you need is love." Obviously, I didn't sing with the Beatles, but I was in the car with the windows up or in the shower when nobody was around, and I sang. The tune and the words stuck. It seemed so simple and so true. That is, all you need is love. In his opening verses, James calls upon the church to be mature and complete. James knows mature and complete love comes from God. The Bible says, "God is love" (I John 4:16). Spiritual knowledge informs us that God is the source of love.

For me, the words of the Beatles song have mellowed over the years, and I no longer sing but reflect on the words, "all you need is God." In fact, love actually needs God. Love needs a rule or a ruler. It is how vows are made and how love becomes sacred. Love can't go it alone. Love on its own is deficient or incomplete. I have seen love when it spins out of control and when it becomes destructive and immature. To this understanding of a mature love, James writes the church to receive God's love which, "is lacking in nothing" (James 1:4).

Rather than dwell on what the church needs, he is convinced the church—regardless of size or denomination—

has everything needed. Instead of dwelling on the problems of the church, he encourages us to look forward to where we are headed and mean what we pray for God's kingdom—to come here on earth, just as in heaven. Sure, the church has concerns, but the empty tomb signals God's invitation to receive life in Christ and live a restored life of love like never before.

As we let such a message from James permeate, we experience a knee-jerk reaction that pushes back and sees only the shortcomings of the church—the limits, the weaknesses, and not the gifts. I know. I have lived it.

I think about how many meetings I sat through with finance committees and watched the wringing of hands over balancing a budget. The word "more" really got old. It seemed like we always needed more. More people. More money. The maintenance and property issues cried out for more attention. The staff who surrounded and supported me needed more of an increase for budget requests and salaries. On top of administrative issues, daily pastoral concerns cried for more. Then, I would go home and wonder how I was to pay for my children's college education, which every year costs more and more. As I read James, I think, "lacking in nothing." Seriously?

By the way, these are first world, middle-class concerns. We find it hard to imagine Christians throughout the world who have no food and who go hungry from day to day. Their water is dirty. Housing is only as good as the boards and tin that survived the last hurricane. And for someone like Sirata, the dangers of martyrdom and violence are as close as her father-in-law who regularly beats her for converting from Buddhism to Christianity.[1] That is only a look at issues within the church.

If the message of James is hard to accept within the church, consider how young people perceive the church from the outside. They are running from the church today because, according to Barna Research, 85 percent of them who have had exposure to Christians and churches have the impression present day Christianity is *hypocritical*. And if you want to pile on negative images, 87 percent of young adults say the term *judgmental* accurately describes present-day Christianity.[2]

Now we get back to the notion the church is lacking in nothing. James boldly claims two gifts for the church, and both stand as important reminders for the faith community then as today. The two gifts James identifies are maturity and completeness. That does not give us license to think we have it all together and "look at us, all buttoned-up" as mature and complete. It is not about looks. It is about a goal, a biblical standard, a priority to become mature and complete in Christ. It doesn't mean we are better or worse than the person down the block. It simply means in Christ we have direction, purpose, and meaning that provides an understanding of character formation that is valued.

First, begin with maturity and the importance it has for the church. Maturity forms and shapes the unique character of the emotional and intellectual relationships for all who walk through our church doors.

GIFT ONE: BE MATURE

When considering young adults and their complaint that the church is hypocritical and judgmental, think for a moment of what parents are going through these days. Raising kids is not easy in our contemporary society. We read about everything from controlling "helicopter parents" to Yale law professor Amy Chua's claim that "Tiger Moms" create a household with strict, Chinese discipline. Parental control seems a greater concern than ever.

Adding to these concerns, problems with everything from eating disorders to early drug and alcohol abuse to the effects of poverty stunt the emotional and physical growth of children. Parents are confused and conflicted by the demands placed on their household these days and especially with respect to children who are either growing too fast or who seem stunted in their growth and not advancing fast enough. Underlying this discussion, of course, lies the deeper concern of maturity.

As a long-term pastor, I observed a common consensus within the mainstream church that when children grew up and left the church, they would come back once they married and had children. The problem arose when these young adults went off to college and never returned, or when they did, they postponed marriage and delayed having children even further. Church, and the idea of coming back, were not on the radar. Again, in Barna's research, the cultural shift and landscape is overwhelming, with secularization on the rise and the attitudes of young adults changing. In George Barna and David Kinnaman's book, *Churchless*, data shows over half this population is unchurched. If the church today is designed to nurture spiritual growth and faith development, we are missing a large segment of our population.

Psychological and sociological inquiries, made by pioneers such as Eric Erickson, Daniel Levinson, Jean Piaget, and Lawrence Kohlberg, have provided constructs and theories that examine the stages of development from infancy to later adulthood. In different ways, all have influenced schools of thought and followers who further brought great insight and teaching to physical, intellectual, emotional, and social maturity. James Fowler is best known for examining the stages of faith development that further enhance the research and concerns many have today with our younger generation.

This age group consumes massive amounts of information found on their smartphones from any subject before they graduate from middle school. Yet, the problem remains that, as advanced as these young people appear, many are missing marks of maturity necessary for growing both autonomy and responsibility. As author Dr. Tim Elmore concludes:

1. Children are overexposed to information, far earlier than they're ready.
2. Children are underexposed to real-life experiences far later than they're ready.[3]

Maturity and the development or growth of faith requires spiritual knowledge. Such knowledge is different from the academic mastering of facts and figures. Spiritual knowledge is based on a relationship in Christ that interacts within his kingdom. Christ is our advocate. An advocate (Latin *ad-vocare,* to call) is one who calls. It is also one who has our backs and defends. Jesus refers to us by saying "I *know* my own and my own know me." (John 10:14, emphasis added). The relationship in Christ is reciprocal. It involves both the cross and the resurrection. Our knowledge in Christ comes from hard knocks but we also find it in times of joy.

This is a relationship that cannot be taken away from us. As a result, we mature in Christ and when and if we are distracted or stumble or even find ourselves confused and conflicted by decisions we have made or are about to make, we find people in church with the knowledge we seek. These people are faithful Christians. They are in church. And they may be at home.

AUNT ANISE AND TERESSA OF AVILA

I think often of the down home wisdom and maturity of my great-aunt in south central Kentucky. Aunt Anise had an old, covered water well in her backyard, which was absolutely amazing to a suburban Chicago kid like me. She also wrung chickens by the neck, plucked their feathers, and cooked the best chicken with biscuits and gravy long before Colonel Sanders started his fast food business.

She was as country as you can get. But she knew her Bible, and she knew her Lord, Jesus. I gained sayings from her that I remember to this day, such as "well, bless my soul," or "mercy, mercy me." Most of all, I appreciated her willingness to sit and listen. As a young boy, I wasn't much of a talker, but her presence was enough. I recall she had no television in her house. Instead, a big swing hung on the front porch where we sat while she shucked beans, and we talked for hours. I consider Anise my first spiritual mentor. It was what today we call "soul-care." At an any early age, I sought what she knew about Jesus, and our relationship was a source of knowledge. She became a spiritual mentor by forming my character in Christ as well as a deep desire for spiritual maturity within me.

For contemporary readers, consider the mysticism as well of the sixteenth century book, *The Interior Castle*, by Saint Teresa of Avila. Today, it might be a chore to read, especially for those who have not engaged in classical readings or given serious thought to the work of the soul. Yet as we read her majestic work, we begin "to think of the soul as if it were a castle made of a single diamond."[4] She writes profoundly about the seven mansions found within the soul and what Christians find as they make their way entering and discovering the various rooms and dangers that await their journey. Her understanding of the soul and the continued progress is likened to a silkworm who, after much toil and labor, emerges as a beautiful butterfly and is endowed with a spirit of God. Growth is found in the interior castle as a way of describing the maturing process of the Christian. Teresa's writing is yet another source of spiritual knowledge.

The mature church is a sacred place and space where our job, like that of Aunt Anise and Teressa, is to discover the many mansions found within people of the church. Christians, like a silkworm, are designed by our very nature to grow and change and be transformed, but along the way, we flower and bear fruit. A natural sign of a church seeking this maturity in Christ will not be hypocrisy but rather be "known by their fruits." (Matthew 7:16).

Jesus states, "This is eternal life, that they may know you, the only true God, and Jesus Christ whom you have sent" (John 17:3). Such eternal knowledge is about as mature and complete as it gets. A relationship with Christ makes it so. The thought of being complete makes it natural to consider now the second gift James claims for the church.

Gift Two: Be Complete

James encourages us to set a priority on becoming mature in the love of Christ, which will remind us of the reality that we are "lacking in nothing" and furthermore assures we are complete in Christ. "May you be mature and complete," James writes. For those unfamiliar with James, we find many verses, phrases, and parallels to the Sermon on the Mount in his letter. Although James may be using expressions from Jesus shared through an early oral tradition, he undoubtably also wrote from memory and his firsthand knowledge of the very words Jesus spoke. We know James and Jesus were in the same family and they traveled together, walked together, ate together and obviously held conversations together. Worthwhile is our consideration that Jesus said much of what he had to say while here on earth in the presence of James.

We do not know if James actually witnessed Jesus preaching the Sermon on the Mount. Nor do we know if the Sermon on the Mount was delivered in the way Matthew recorded it or like the wording found in the gospel of Luke or simply a compilation of an oral tradition that was passed to the gospel writers from earlier sources. All this begs the question of how close James was to the original wording and meaning found in the Sermon on the Mount.

Much of this discussion comprises a field in which scholars cultivate new insights and theories and academic research. But this much is certain, the Letter of James is the first writing filled with quotes and sayings that parallel the Sermon on the Mount. And these same sayings are found later in both Matthew and Luke and their respective versions of the Sermon on the Mount.

We can pinpoint James as the earliest source for the church to both witness and understand the priority of discipleship and spiritual formation. James speaks to us directly from the words of Jesus. They are words of authority carried from generation to generation. They are words that must be part of the vocabulary within the church especially today.

For example, in Matthew's Gospel, Jesus preaches about the important matter of social relationships and the connection this has with God. Jesus talks about anger and adultery. We get it. But then he brings up divorce—not as a separate matter—but as a continuation of anger spiraling out of control. Jesus also speaks on making oaths and covenants and promises. What happens when these agreements break apart? We see a desire for retaliation and hatred which turns people into enemies and opens the door for evil. What begins with anger escalates quickly into a spiritual conflict between good and evil. In response to this slippery slope, Jesus says to his listeners "Be perfect, therefore, as your heavenly Father is perfect" (Matthew 5:48).

Be perfect. Here again, our response might be "really?" When in the throes of anger, few of us consider being perfect, much less have perfect thoughts. When promises are broken, when marriages dissolve, every word but "perfect" rises to the surface. Anger can separate us from our neighbor and from God. However, anger is not the sin. Anger is a serious warning that something is amiss.

Recall when Jesus kneels next to the woman who committed adultery. He tells the gang of self-righteous Pharisees with stones in their hands, "Let anyone among you who is without sin, be the first to throw a stone at her" (John 8:7). We know the rest of the story—the men walked away, and the woman was set free of sin.

Or remember when Jesus says, "Woe to you scribes and Pharisees, hypocrites! For you clean the outside of the cup and of the plate, but inside [you] are full of greed and self-indulgence" (Matthew 23:25). Jesus clearly does not like hypocrisy, and he questions those who appear good on the outside but are covering-up what they are honestly thinking and feeling within.

Yet, James calls on the church to be "complete" by applying the same word Jesus uses when calling on us to be "perfect" as our heavenly Father is perfect. Once again, Barna Research finds only "15 percent of young adults outside the church thought the lifestyles of Christ followers were significantly different from the norm."[5]

Often, we miss the layered understanding of the word "perfect" or "complete" which is derived from the Greek word *teleioi* meaning "finished." Some may recognize the philosophical word "teleological" or Aristotle's use of the word "telos," which reflects not only our purpose for existing but more importantly, the conclusion or final goal—that is, how we finish. With that in mind, when the church hears Jesus's cry, "it is finished" (John 19:30) from the cross, the word *teleo* is used as the final word that his life is "perfect," or "complete."

In this one moment, the atonement—the offering of Jesus—takes place. The sacrifice given to God elicits faith on the part of the church. The world is now perfectly, completely, finally reconciled to God in Christ. Jesus has broken the power of sin. Faith in Christ puts us in a right relationship with God. Neither we nor the church is perfect, complete, or finished, but God makes the work of reconciliation and restoring the dignity of our life with him possible through the sacrifice of Jesus. His sacrifice completes his work which sets in context the remarkable witness James provides for the church that is, "lacking in nothing."

I Am the Bread of Life

As mentioned previously, many scholars now date the Letter of James as one of the earliest Christian writings. It appeared in 47-49 AD, which fits with a time of famine and severe economic, social, and religious upheavals.[6] As also noted, the Letter of James contains frequent parallels to the Sermon on the Mount and other sayings of Jesus found in the synoptic gospels. It's easy to overlook the theological emphasis James provides for spiritual growth within the early church. James and the evangelist John led the early church in Jerusalem. Recall Jesus on the cross crying out to John, saying "Here is your mother." From that hour, John took Mary into his home (John 19:27). This may have been the earliest church in Jerusalem, and James was considered the pillar. James and John both gave shape to the early belief structure of the early church.

By writing to the church "lacking in nothing" (James 1:4) during a societal time of harsh deprivation rekindles the memory of faith. James rekindles the memory of faith by instilling within the church, the sufficiency of Jesus, who says, "I AM the bread of life" (John 6:35).

This description of Jesus as the bread of life speaks on many levels, but in the gospel story, it immediately lifts the imagination and the image of Jesus himself as food for the hungry, one who responds to those in need so they "shall not want" (Psalm 23:1). As the bread of life, Jesus comes down from heaven and feeds us with ample provisions and an abundance of life with God. This life differs from our mortal, human, limited existence in a natural life. Life with God is real and is anything but an escape from reality. Jesus, the bread of life, describes the reality of life with God within his kingdom:

> Our ancestors ate the manna in the wilderness; as it is written, "He gave them bread from heaven to eat." Then Jesus said to them, "Very truly, I tell you, it was not

Moses who gave you the bread from heaven, but it was my Father who gives you the true bread from heaven. For the bread of God is that which comes down from heaven and gives life to the world." They said to him, "Sir, give us this bread always." Jesus said to them, "I am the bread of life." (John 6: 31-35)

Recall that Moses, prior to the wilderness journey, asked God to identify himself, and God thundered back, "I AM WHO I AM" (Exodus 3:14). This is the biblical description and term that profoundly expresses not only the existence of God but the essence of God. God is not physical or limited or even defined by simply his substance, but rather God makes himself manifest by his spiritual presence that enters our world—like the essence of bread. Jesus further clarifies this understanding of God's presence by saying to his disciples, "It was not Moses who gave you the bread from heaven, but it is my Father who gives you the true bread from heaven" (John 6:32).

The bread—this manna—comes from God. It is not merely about the bread. It is about the presence of God— the essence that nurtures us—in the bread. God provides for the Israelites during their years in the wilderness. It rains down upon them daily. It meets their need for the day. But the bread did not last. According to Scripture, the bread turned foul and contained worms by the next day. Again, God gives more bread with the understanding they must rely on God, and not simply the bread.

When Jesus further unfolds the miraculous Exodus story, he reminds the disciples "your ancestors ate the manna in the wilderness, and they died" (John 6:49). In other words, there is more to life than daily existence. What about our essence? To this, Jesus says, "I am the living bread that came down from heaven. Whoever eats of this bread will live forever" (John 6:51).

This understanding of eating bread—consuming, digesting—describes spiritual formation. The process is experiential, involving all our senses including our spiritual sixth sense. This self-disclosure Jesus makes, "I am the bread of life," helps the disciples see the "sign" of bread in a tangible way as representing and presenting Jesus. It becomes clear Jesus comes from God and enters our existence and the essence of our spiritual being by providing us with life eternal.

The Eucharist is a sacrament, meaning it is sacred. Our eating bread **during Holy Communion** constitutes an outward sign of the inward grace that we are not simply human beings who are consuming something spiritual, but we are spiritual beings who are nourishing and feeding our life with God through the real presence of Jesus Christ. And so, in the Eucharist, we literally give thanks for Emmanuel—God with us—and for a life with God that lacks nothing but is complete and mature in Christ.

James asks, "Can a fig tree, my brothers and sisters yield olives, or a grapevine, figs?" (James 3:12) The church can only produce what it is made to grow. By producing maturity, we lack nothing. James provides the church with a bold witness. But as we might suspect, his witness becomes even greater as we turn our attention to the place of prayer that asks in faith and never doubts.

CHAPTER SUMMARY

- Love needs God. Love needs a rule or a ruler. It is how vows are made and how love becomes sacred. Love can't go it alone. Love on its own is deficient or incomplete. To this understanding of mature love, James writes that a mature church expresses God's love, which "is lacking in nothing" (James 1:4).

- The letter of James identifies two gifts the church is called to claim not merely for ourselves, but as a necessary witness for this next generation. The two gifts are maturity and completeness. Both gifts are necessary for love, and they respond to acts of immaturity and a life that is incomplete.
- Maturity has to do with character formation and knowing God at a deep, personal level that forms a relationship and results in an interaction and intimacy with the sacred in life. Jesus refers to such knowing when he says, "I *know* my own and my own *know* me" (John 10:14, emphasis added). We mature in Christ not by observing but by relating to him. Hence, the need for intergenerational spiritual mentors today. The second gift is complete which means finished. This speaks to not only our purpose for existing but how we finish.
- Jesus says, "I AM the bread of life," which is the sacramental way God enters our existence and the essence of our spiritual being by providing us with a life that is mature and complete and eternal in Christ.

A Spiritual Exercise: The Call

I. A vocation is often thought of in terms of a career, occupation, or profession. It often can be thought of as how you get paid. The problem with that understanding of vocation comes when you enjoy other aspects of your life that have nothing to do with money. Volunteer work, social activities, sports, raising your kids, all make the understanding of vocation something deeper than simply a job.

Who has God created me to be?

II. Another aspect of calling is that it has to do with making a difference. Jesus calls fishermen by saying to them "Follow me, and I will make you fish for people." (Matthew 4:19) The call means you will make a difference in the lives of people. It also means you will follow Jesus, which means as well, Jesus leads.

What might it mean for you to follow Jesus?

III. One aspect of following Jesus means a change or transformation will occur. For each person, it is as different and unique as the calling itself. That should not make it hard to describe. This unfolding of life is autobiographical and needs to be discussed. In a sense, this is the heart of the matter. Where Jesus will lead is not always clear, but it is apparent a spiritual movement is at work. There is a gift waiting to be discovered. So, for now, think about:

What more does Jesus expect of me?

Keeping a journal at this point may be helpful not as a chore or one more thing to do, but rather as a way of bringing into reality some of the thoughts, ideas, and images that are beginning to surface. If you are so inclined, make notes on the three questions above. Pay attention to the conversations, experiences during the week, television, news, worship—you name it—everything is fair game, especially as your life begins to respond to these questions. You need not stay up writing until the wee hours. Make an entry. One paragraph is plenty. Date it. In time, you might go back to the entry and look for a pattern or where God may be at work in your life: **Before we can do the work of God, God needs to work in us.**

CHAPTER 6

PRAYER

"ASK IN FAITH"

(JAMES 1:6)

In the introduction of his letter, James identifies praying in faith as another key attribute of the church. That may seem obvious. But consider praying without faith. Faithless prayer is a wish, a last resort, closing your eyes and crossing your fingers. Praying without faith is child's play. Faithless prayer is ultimately asking, but not really expecting an answer.

Praying in faith is a serious matter. By speaking truth to power, faith conveys a sense of courage, commitment, and confidence. Faith is not for the weak-kneed nor the indecisive. For James and for the early church, faith was pure and simple—life in Jesus Christ. When believers pray, they ask Jesus for guidance, direction, and help as we follow him. Prayer is specific and intentional and finds an answer.

Praying this way is not simply showing faith *for* Jesus. Praying demonstrates faith *in* Jesus. Interactive and personal, faith results in prayer that brings knowledge. We increasingly know Jesus at a deeper level, and we find prayer is not a last resort but a first resource. As an outcome, our praying through faith in Jesus opens us and reveals a relational knowledge (Greek: *ginōskō*) that is far stronger than doubt.

Faith in Jesus and the knowledge of truth hold hands and walk closely together. James encourages the church always to "ask in faith, never doubting" (James 1:6), because truth forms knowledge of what is real, and faith in Jesus is built upon trust in this reality. Faith and trust, like faith and truth, work together and become nearly synonymous. Think for a moment of a marriage where an extramarital affair occurs. The affair damages the marriage relationship not simply because of the sexual activity, but at a far deeper level, it destroys trust. Faith in one another shatters. Granted this is a negative, sad example, but also an explosive reminder of the importance and connection found between faith and trust. This also brings to the surface the unseemly, demeaning nature of doubt.

Some think of doubt as nothing more than healthy skepticism, or they find doubt motivates and helps in thinking through difficult and complex situations. In fact, participants in strategic planning sessions oftentimes consider doubt a basic principle in developing best practices. They use "what if" analysis to vet or "shoot holes" in a proposal and evaluate from top to bottom the strengths and weaknesses of certain ideas and assumptions. Proponents believe doubt constitutes a necessary part of critical thinking.

James writes to a church not engaged in strategic planning but already occupied in "doing the Word." Doubt has no place once a commitment and bond are established. The bond—the covenantal agreement which we hold dearly—unites and joins the church by the power of the cross. With the cross, we consider no "what if." The cross has no room for doubt.

Metaphorically Speaking

To the character of the church and the attributes of prayer asking in faith, James adds this metaphor "For the one who doubts is like a wave of the sea, driven and tossed by the wind, being double-minded and unstable in every way" (James 1:6). This powerful nautical image requires little explanation for the seafaring. James describes an image of a turbulent, swirling body of water, difficult to navigate and undependable. It is unsafe. Life aboard is out of control.

The same holds true for the person who is double-minded. This metaphor further drives home the danger doubt brings with uncertainty and instability. James raises the deep concern about "double-mindedness in every way," which influences the way we think, feel, speak, and act. **This ambivalence** impacts every dimension of our lives. A wavering person is unreliable, uncertain of the direction and the way the path leads. Imagine for a moment driving a car and feeling uncertain of the destination to which you might be headed. James employs this same logic to encourage the church not to doubt the direction but "trust in the Lord with all your heart, and do not rely on your own insight. In all your ways acknowledge him, and he will make straight your paths" (Proverbs 3:5-6).

I Am the Way

Recall it was the disciple John who took Mary the mother of Jesus into his home following the crucifixion. Here a small gathering of Jesus-worshippers gathered, and according to the oral tradition, reflected upon the I AM passages that are familiar today as recorded in John's gospel. Like treasured crystal, we hold and examine these passages with utmost care, but we also realize they are anything but fragile. These I AM sayings are statements of faith that boldly stand throughout the ages.

John recalls one of these I AM expressions within the poignant context of the upper room on the night Jesus was betrayed. Peter says, "Lord, why can I not follow you now? I will lay down my life for you." Jesus answered, "Will you lay down your life for me? Very truly, I tell you, before the cock crows, you will have denied me three times." (John 13:37-38) Here the word "denial" reveals Peter's doubt.

This doubt as revealed by Peter, or what Jesus refers to as you of "little faith" causes obvious pain. Of course, Peter is not the only one whose knees begin to buckle. In the same upper room, we hear the cry of Thomas, "Lord, we do not know where you are going. How can we know the way?" (John 14:5). In this turbulent sea of doubt that is driven by the wind of fear and swirling around and within those of the upper room, Jesus is the captain of the ship. In this upper room of uncertainty, Jesus encourages the disciples by saying, "Do not let your hearts be troubled. Believe in God, believe also in me" (John 14:1). Jesus knows a troubled heart is an unstable heart. It can drive and toss the body around, much like the wind taking a ship off course where it loses direction in unchartered waters.

Jesus in the upper room clearly and eloquently personalizes faith, truth, and the knowledge of reality and sets it on the Passover table when he says to the disciples, to the church, and to all generations: "I am the way, and the truth, and the life. No one comes to the Father except through me" (John 14:6).

To our darkened eyes, Jesus becomes the lighthouse, flashing the light of safety and direction through the fog of doubt and the churning fear. Jesus is the way, the one who calms the troubled heart. And he adds these words: "If you know me, you will know my Father also" (John 14:7). To all those tossed about by the waves of doubt, Jesus provides direction, meaning, and purpose, even during the storm like the one swirling here in the upper room. Whenever doubt enters, we find room for Jesus who is the Way.

Jesus clearly and unambiguously takes command, and he invites us to place our confidence in him with hearts that are now calm and set on following Jesus all the way. This single-mindedness is the source of our salvation, and it is the "sure and steadfast anchor of the soul" (Hebrews 6:19). Faith, truth, and the knowledge of reality converge in the upper room, as humanity sees the way toward a living God who holds out the arms of rescue and salvation.

The early church was known for believers who were so dependent upon this single-minded understanding of faith in Jesus they became nicknamed a people of "the Way" (Acts 9:2). Obviously, a Roman culture with a plethora of gods and goddesses had a hard time believing the notion of placing faith in a crucified man or even one god. The many gods of the Parthenon in Greece stood as a longstanding tribute to the tradition of speculation and the fluidity early philosophers held when it came to the matter of faith. They believed in not one way but many ways to appease the gods and calm a troubled heart. This disdain for the exclusivity of one way as revealed in Jesus echoes down through the ages to the pluralism of our day.

EXCLUSIVITY AND WISDOM

The Barna Group documents a negative perception the church holds for young adults today. By studying the attitudes, values, and developing beliefs of young people in depth, the research center concludes one of the most pervasive criticisms this next generation claims is the exclusive nature of the church. They perceive a club-like atmosphere in the church—a secret society or a special handshake—that somehow makes one acceptable. To those who are exploring the Christian faith, young people experience an "insider-outsider" mentality, which opposes their value of tolerance. The need for tolerance is considered the North Star for many young adults.[1] Diversity then follows. Young people are saying if the church is to have any appeal for the spiritual lives of millions of today's twenty-somethings, it needs to drop the notion of single-mindedness and become more open-minded. The idea that one faith holds the absolute truth is off-putting.

Here James instructs the church "if any of you is lacking in wisdom, ask God who gives to all generously" (1:5) Rather than heaping more criticism upon the church,

James emphasizes the need to seek wisdom while faithfully living in a changing culture. James saw this first-hand by observing Jesus who, "increased in wisdom and in years and in divine and human favor" (Luke 2:52).

Jesus came often into conflict with the religious authorities, using wisdom in his defense. When Jesus ate with tax collectors, the scribes criticized him for associating with the unclean, to which Jesus responded, "those who are well have no need of a physician" (Mark 2:17). In another instance, the disciples plucked grain on the Sabbath and were denounced. To this, Jesus replied, "The sabbath was made for humankind, and not humankind for the sabbath" (Mark 2:27).

Jesus applied wisdom when rejected and stressed to his disciples this wisdom emerged from the center of his life and spirit, which he confirmed by saying, "Take my yoke upon you, and learn from me; for I am gentle and humble in heart" (Matthew 11:29).

Another word for gentleness is meekness. One resource for wisdom is this understanding of meekness. Meekness protects the truth. Rather than hurling the gospel truth around in arrogance or retaliating with a mean spirit, meekness provides restraint. With a quiet confidence, the church is to ask God for wisdom in facing criticism, more so persecution (James 1:5). By inviting the church into a life of wisdom, we promote the truth—but in meekness. Truth and faith in Jesus merge in a witness of profound wisdom and the development of a character that does not overreact. In a pluralistic age of instant information and high-speed technology, wisdom and meekness are welcomed companions to the profound gospel truth.

I AM THE TRUTH

Jesus makes the claim that he is not only the way, but he is the truth. Again, such a claim seems to push the younger generation further from the church, especially with the following verse: "No one comes to the Father except through me" (John 14:6). This, of course, is where the label of "exclusivity" tends to empty the pews and silence the pulpits. Again, a little wisdom goes a long way.

We know truth, by its very nature, is in and of itself exclusive. Everything is not—nor can everything be—true. Therefore, some things are not true.

Point being, if everything is true, acceptable, and correct, then nothing is wrong or false or dishonest. In such a world, there would be no such thing as a lie or deceit or wrongdoing because, don't forget, everything is true. Of course, truth is based on knowledge and reality— we know dishonesty, deception, and evil exist. Those who tell us the church is being exclusive for believing Jesus is the only truth then push the church outside the circle of reason and claim the church is unreasonable. In other words, truth becomes a cultural struggle where lines are quickly drawn. Here again, God provides the spiritual gift of wisdom and the blessing of meekness, as James knows, when we pray by "asking in faith" (James 1:6).

First, wisdom reminds us truth—possessing the truth, knowing the truth, confessing the truth—is not a bad thing. In fact, the Christian tradition finds truth liberating. As Jesus says, "If you continue in my word, you are truly my disciples; and you will know the truth, and the truth will make you free" (John 8:32). If we consider the opposite of not knowing the truth, we find ourselves in bondage. We might recall the old TV show, *Truth or Consequences*. James clearly wants the church to stand for truth as revealed in Jesus Christ because knowledge, faith, and reality are all revealed in the truth of Jesus. When the light of truth does not shine, darkness is the consequence.

Secondly, if holding the truth is not a bad thing, then it is fair to profess truth as a good thing. When we refer to the truth as a good thing, we can also consider truth to be a God thing. By bringing God into the discussion of truth, we become acutely aware of the force who opposes the light of truth in God—the devil, the darkness, and the father of lies. As an example, in Kentucky, the judge tells us to "raise your right hand and tell the truth—so help you God." This makes a strong point that we can rely upon the truth. If we do not tell the truth, not only will we be held in contempt of court, but we will mislead, trick, and deceive others by falsehood. The church is designed by its nature to be reasonable and in communion with God by housing the body of Christ and, therefore, witnessing to the gospel truth. It is one of our attributes or characteristics. The truth of Jesus is in our DNA. It is who we are.

Finally, wisdom and meekness wrap around truth, and they stand before the cross. The church does not hold up truth in a triumphal, arrogant way but rather lifts truth high upon the cross. Nailed to the cross hangs our Lord and Savior, pummeled by sin, evil, and death—to the delight of the devil. At the foot of the cross, our prayers are lifted up in the faith of the resurrection, and we never doubt but know "the fear of the Lord is the beginning of wisdom" (Proverbs 9:10).

The fear of the Lord does not mean the Lord is frightening, nor does it mean the church is afraid. Rather, fear reveals the holiness of the Lord, who is the beginning of wisdom. The Holy Spirit, whose holiness opens us to the truth, gives the church the gift of wisdom. The Spirit invites us to receive this truth with meekness that leads to wisdom. We learn of this meekness in the Sermon on the Mount as Jesus blesses the multitudes with the beatitude, "Blessed are the meek, for they will inherit the earth." (Matthew 5:5). David Kinnaman simply concludes his study on the next generation and the challenge presented to the church by writing, "Wisdom empowers us to live faithfully in a changing culture."[2]

I Am the Life

Meekness is not a sign of weakness. Nor does it result from a subservient attitude by a person who avoids conflict and sidesteps disagreement. The church, in meekness and wisdom, stands before the cross and before the truth of God and sees only holiness. Holy because the cross represents a life dependent upon God and God alone. Holy because we see in the cross not death but life. Life with God, a life that is ever-lasting, immortal, and an eternal destiny in the kingdom of God.

On the cross, Jesus cries out the words of the psalmist "Eli, Eli, lama sabachthani?" (Matthew 27:46) translated as "My God, my God, why has thou forsaken me?" (Psalm 22:1) Some hear this cry as a pitiful complaint, as if God has abandoned Jesus. Others hear in this moan of despair and resignation the silence of a God who has not only left Jesus to die but is nowhere to be found. Still others looking at the cross see nothing more than a tragic defeat. For such observers of the crucifixion, it is over. And to them, God seems powerless.

Of course, the early Christians heard and saw something entirely different. There on the cross, clear and simple, bloody and broken, Jesus was able to ask in faith, never doubting. The psalm Jesus quotes recalls intense suffering and seems to fulfill the experience of Jesus on the cross. In the end, Jesus's question heightens his deliverance and victory as God brings within the context of suffering, the promise of hope.

> To him, indeed, shall all who sleep in the earth bow down; before him shall bow all who go down to the dust, and I shall live for him. Posterity will serve him; future generations will be told about the Lord, and proclaim his deliverance to a people yet unborn, saying that he has done it." (Psalm 22: 29-31)

James writes to the church, "Ask in faith, never doubting" (James 1:6) By never doubting, we are asking in faith and can know the assurance that God "will never leave you nor forsake you" (Hebrews 13:5). As a result, asking God in faith compels us, as well, to listen in faith and hear what God has to say. Meaning God is with us forever. Our life in God is forever. Although on earth for a relatively short time, we listen to Jesus for words that guide and direct us through teachings, parables, healings. Ultimately in his death and resurrection, we hear the very word of God—providing we listen.

LIKE A WISE MAN

The conclusion to the Sermon on the Mount tells of a wise man who hears the words of Jesus and builds his house on the foundation of rock. Jesus compares him to the foolish man who hears the same words but does not want God's guidance and so acts by building his house on sand (Matthew 7:24).

As we listen for Jesus in our life, the parables speak to those who have "ears to hear, let him hear" (Matthew 11:15). Such an announcement is a pronouncement for all who are listening for God's word to be attentive and aware of how God communicates with us through the prayer of faith. It provides specific content and meaning for a variety of situations and experiences that like seeds are planted in the soil and the very soul of our lives. The prayer of faith relates all we do with all God does so his will is done on earth just as in heaven. That is our prayer. It is a prayer the church offers the next generation as we are in communion with God.

God communicates with us through prayer. Should we hear the word of God and not act and not do what we hear, we are nothing more than the foolish builder who built his house on sand and when "the winds blew and beat against that house, and it fell—and great was its fall" (Matthew 7:27).

James identifies prayers asked in faith and never doubting as the attribute he witnesses to by calling us to be "doers of the word, and not merely hearers who deceive themselves" (James 1:22). When we follow Jesus as the way, the truth, and the life, doubt vanishes, and the church, grounded in prayer, is prepared to act with meekness and humbleness of heart. Our identity resides in Christ who will raise us up. This cannot be said for those who busy themselves in gathering their treasure here on earth. Such a life, James tells us, is like a flower which will only wither away. To the plight of the rich, we now turn our attention.

Chapter Summary

- James calls upon the church to pray by asking in faith and never doubting.
- Without faith, prayer is like a wave of the sea, driven and tossed by the wind. It makes for doubt, uncertainty and double-mindedness in every way.
- Faith in Jesus is personalized by the reality of his word, "I AM, the way, and the truth, and the life. No one comes to the Father except through me" (John 14:6). Jesus is the lighthouse and anchor for people of the way.
- Absolute truth conflicts with a generation that values inclusivity, tolerance, and diversity. Yet, Jesus is "meek and lowly of heart" (Matthew 11:29 KJV).
- Meekness and wisdom are wrapped in truth and stand together at the cross. The prayer of faith relates all we do with all God does, so his will is done on earth just as it is in heaven. The church must pray for the next generation.

A Spiritual Exercise

A Personal Experience of John 14:6

This is an exercise to help you begin to look at the important spiritual developments in your life. Jesus says, "I AM the **way**, the **truth** and the **life**" (John 14:6 emphasis added). Take a few moments and chart your experiences through the years of faith or the lack thereof. Recall times where the *way*, was blessed, with gifts of joy, love, and the presence of the holy or sacred. Identify those high times on the left.

On the right, identify times of challenge, crisis, or doubt that occurred on the way.

Go back and circle a truth you learned from the incident on either the left or right.

Finally, underline the experiences that still have an importance for you today. How might the way, truth, and life you have lived to this point, reflect an intimacy or listening to Jesus, God, or the Holy Spirit?

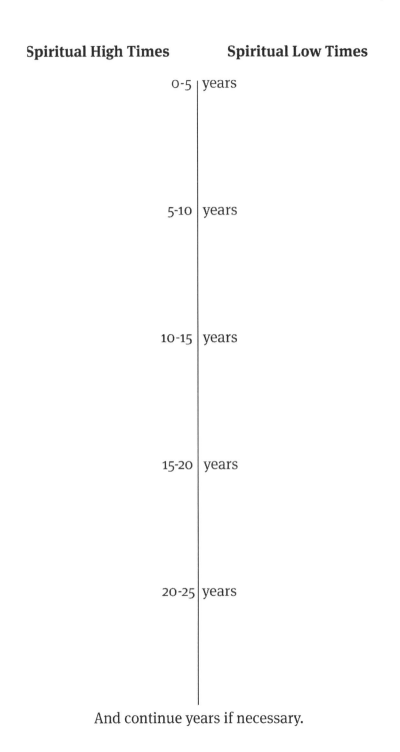

Spiritual High Times   **Spiritual Low Times**

0-5 | years

5-10 | years

10-15 | years

15-20 | years

20-25 | years

And continue years if necessary.

CHAPTER 7

SHOW NO PARTIALITY

"THE RICH WILL DISAPPEAR"

(JAMES 1:10)

I will never forget looking over my bank statement after Christmas one year. My credit card usually balloons at that time of the year, but it seemed to list more charges and excessive amounts than I could account for. Santa was good, but this was a little ridiculous. I sat down with my wife to have a heart-to-heart without totally losing my cool. Like me, however, she could not explain some of the entries, and they appeared not only in December. As we started going back through November and October, we found more and more unusual charges. You probably guessed it by now. We were victims of fraud. Our credit card had been used for unauthorized purchases.

When I reported this to the bank, they cancelled our card immediately, then reimbursed the fraudulent charges on the next month's statement and issued another credit card. It seemed like just another day for the bank. But I was traumatized. I became somewhat paranoid as I began to question that if my credit card was stolen, what other personal information of mine floated out there in the dark cyber world? I had been robbed. A thief broke into my account and stole.

James writes to the church, "the rich will disappear like a flower in the field." Jesus initially issued this warning when he spoke within the context of the Sermon on the Mount. Jesus called upon his followers to change priorities and think seriously about organizing life around God and not the material world of mammon and riches.

Seek first the kingdom of God means we are not to pursue only the treasures of this world but prioritize by treasuring God first in our heart. Jesus reminds us to consider the birds of the air and the lilies of the field as examples—not of self-reliance but of relying upon the nature of God, the creator. By trusting God as the treasure of our lives and not merely the things of this world, Jesus calls for a fundamental shift among his followers. It is more than telling them just to "keep it simple."

TREASURE GOD

As a follower of Jesus, James naturally reiterates this same caution with possessions. James speaks further to the bitter irony and the fine line that appears when rather than possessing treasures, we become possessed by them. This is a serious matter of the heart and to this concern, James writes

> Your riches have rotted, and your clothes are moth-eaten. Your gold and silver have rusted, and their rust will be evidence against you, and it will eat your flesh like fire. You have laid up treasure for the last day. (James 5:2-3)

Priorities, values, and spiritual life reveal themselves by who—or what—opens our hearts. Daily prayer, reflection, and a response is required before it is too late. Death will bring an end to life, even for those who treasure wealth and whose hearts belong to this world. James is not making a hard-nosed attack on prosperity. Rather, he conveys a deeper understanding of misappropriation. Taking what has been given to us and misusing it amounts to poor stewardship. Recall from Genesis that we are made in the image of God, which is not a reflection of how we look on the outside but rather an image of God's insight into how we manage, organize, and appear within. James wants the church to know that anything other than treasuring our relationship with God equates to mismanagement and leads to nothing but a broken heart.

In the Sermon on the Mount, Jesus first speaks of this priority when he appeals to his followers "Do not store up for yourselves treasures on earth ... but store up for yourselves treasures in heaven" (Matthew 6:19-20). This is the abundant life to which Jesus refers. Like a cup, abundance with God overflows (Psalm 23), and it can be lived now by treasuring God first and foremost. As with anything valuable, we protect the purpose, meaning, and worth of God.

Granted, there may be those who think God does not need protection. But we do need to protect our relationship with God and defend this gift, because this precious asset connects us to our spirit, dignity, and heart. We keep this treasure safe—but not necessarily locked in a safe.

For example, I wear a wedding ring. My wife gave it to me as a gift from her grandfather. On the ring, the couple's initials are engraved and the date 1905—the year her grandparents were married. It tells quite a story. More importantly, now it represents my responsibility to protect, guard, and defend the vows I made when I married my wife. I wear the ring in public rather than store it in a lockbox because it's not private. The ring symbolizes my public commitment and speaks not only to me but to anyone who sees it. It signifies a life of love made available to me from the day of our wedding forward. I share this example not of wealth but of a treasure that is in my heart and which I zealously guard.

THERE YOUR HEART WILL BE

Recall the conclusion Jesus reaches when saying, "where your treasure is, there your heart will be also"

(Matthew 6:21). James no doubt heard Jesus speak these sayings regarding the heart and treasure firsthand. He knew faith in Christ provided a bridge to the gap between the rich and poor. James knew God bestowed no partiality, no favoritism, no privilege. Only blessings awaited those who treasured God. Again, this single-minded focus on "the Way" affirms proper character over greed and begs the inner, spiritual question: "Who is really a good person?"[1] The response to such a question taps into where gifts, talents, and competencies join the heart by opening us to the love and calling of God.

I remember going as part of the leadership team on a mission trip to the Dominican Republic with our church's youth group. Our third son, John, traveled with me. The mission opened his eyes to the poverty and need surrounding him as soon as we entered a Haitian refugee camp. We all debrief at night and allowed the youth to unpack many of the emotions and experiences that occurred during the day. As a proud parent, I tried not to wink at John or give him a thumbs-up during these discussions. Instead, I did my best to remain somewhat objective and impersonal and not get in his way. We did talk at length on the flight home. I was impressed by the impact the mission had on him and his openness in discussing, in a real way, how God was at work in the camp regardless of the circumstances.

After returning home, I got up early the next morning and was having breakfast with my youngest. John entered the room just as his brother, then around age seven, complained someone had taken the toy out of the cereal box. Without hesitation, John took the box of cereal, grabbed the gallon of milk, and shouted at his seven-year-old brother, "Quit complaining. You don't know how lucky you are!" With that he stormed off, leaving his little brother in tears.

In some respects, the story reminds me of the righteous indignation Jesus displayed when he turned over the money changers' tables in the temple. Though the cereal-box incident isn't quite as sensational, it did take place right before my eyes. I witnessed firsthand the impact a mission makes on the heart no matter the age. Sure, my job as a parent entailed smoothing over some rough edges between the boys after the blowup, but the point remained clear and sharp. When the reality of Jesus meets the culture head on, the calling to serve and to influence the world becomes incredibly powerful. Sometimes that calling manifests itself in a way that brings people back to their senses. They want to live again with a heart for God's desire.

RESILIENT DISCIPLES

David Kinnaman refers to "resilient disciples" within the next generation. This young group of faithful followers have a strong sense of mission and purpose for their lives. Barna Research finds "90 percent want 'others to see Jesus reflected in me through my words and actions.'"[2] Granted, this group of eighteen-to-twenty-nine-year-olds represents only 10 percent of youngsters who grew up as Christians, but they attend church at least once a month, they trust the Bible, they believe in Jesus, and they want to put their faith to work. This is a group that will grow in numbers, and they will be the influencers for a whole new generation. We can't give up on them.

They do not call attention to themselves, nor are they self-righteous or looking for a pat on the back. Mission is a deep calling. They sense God at work in life and possess a longing that seems upside down and counterculture "not to be served but to serve" (Matthew 20:28). At a young age, these Jesus followers know the difference between serving for applause compared to expressing their new identity in Christ by their actions and lifestyle. This next generation also realizes a mission trip out of the country is not always necessary to find God.

These resilient disciples seem to say the need for mission is taking place at home and in the workplace and on the ball field. In other words, they see the need right in front of them. Of course, service and the Gospel and good deeds are required all around the world, but sometimes—oftentimes—the greatest needs are looking right at us. This next generation is not holding its breath waiting for government, big business, or education to fix what is broken and supply what is missing. Rather they see it as their Christian responsibility. Something needs to be done today. They detect a sense of urgency. God has placed this need upon the believer's heart for a reason, and herein lies the call for mission. Their drive is exciting and extreme in a good sense because few others are willing to take the risk. And they are in the church—not of tomorrow, but of today.

I AM THE GATE

Again, we recall the I AM passages from the gospel of John with the understanding that both John's writings and leadership are intimately involved with the early church in Jerusalem. The tenderness James holds for the early church surely came from the moment when Jesus, hanging on the cross, looks out to see his mother and says to John, "Here is your mother. And from that hour the disciple took her into his own home" (John 19: 27). By following the footsteps of John and Jesus's mother home, we find a sacred place that will become a main source and space for the early church in Jerusalem, and where, no doubt, James is a frequent visitor. Following the crucifixion and the resurrection of Jesus and moving into the formation of the early church in Jerusalem with John and Mary, James worships the risen Lord. He provides such a strong witness he is referred to as the "pillar" of the church.

The pillar, a special term used for a church leader, evokes an image of the obvious and necessary architectural stability and strength found within the person. But a pillar also reminds us of Solomon and his Temple where a pillar held the place and sacred space together for all to enter and worship. More importantly, the pillar provides entrance and access to the tabernacle of the Most High. John expands this metaphor of the pillar further when he writes, "I will make you a pillar in the temple of my God" (Revelation 3:12). He refers to the New Jerusalem where the pillar supports the worship and provides access to the angels and archangels and all the company of heaven. And James holds up this eternal vision of church and of worship like a pillar just as the stability of heaven and earth are held together by God.

Images like a pillar give our minds something concrete to grasp that helps with our spiritual formation and growth by providing an understanding of what makes a good person. By placing his trust and faith in Jesus, by treasuring Jesus in his heart, James realizes the highest call is not to store up treasures on earth but to love here on earth and thereby store up treasures in heaven. James puts it like this, "Listen, my beloved brothers and sisters. Has not God chosen the poor in the world to be rich in faith and to be heirs of the kingdom that he has promised to those who love him?" (James 2: 5).

James surely heard the oral saying of Jesus, "Very truly I tell you, I am the gate of the sheep" (John 10:7). Jesus is the gate. Today's sensibilities may question the metaphor of a gate by likening the gate to a barrier, a moat, or a wall, designed only to keep people out. A gate may conjure up an image of a "no trespassing" sign or a chain link fence and a padlock preventing entrance. Some in our culture today may see this imagery as a gated community and a restrictive image. Nothing could be further from the truth.

The gate described by Jesus interweaves with the context of his being the good shepherd and paints the picture of something needed to protect the sheep. It is required to prevent the sheep from wandering. The gate compares to a seat belt used in a car today, a restraint to keep us from getting hurt. The gate is used for good purposes by the good shepherd. But the gate also provides access and entrance. It opens for those whose hearts love God. The gate clarifies the choice we have between our commitments to worldly treasures or to God and the treasures in heaven. It should not be a tough choice, but it is.

Some will recall the story of the rich young ruler who turned away from Jesus because he cared more for his wealth. About this decision, Jesus told his disciples "I tell you, it is easier for a camel to go through the eye of a needle than for someone who is rich to enter the kingdom of God" (Matthew 19:24). Like most, the disciples struggled with such requirements for entrance into the kingdom, wondering out loud who could be saved? After all, the wealthy were the ones supposed to be blessed. And now Jesus blesses the poor. A clear division seemed to be in the making. Which is it? Rich or poor?

THE DOOR TO HUMILITY

Jesus clearly and unequivocally makes the point that it is not about an individual's ability to earn salvation, be they rich or poor. Rather the decision rests with God, whom we are called to treasure, to love, and to serve here and now. Both poor and rich, healthy and sick, lost and found can walk together. We can all join hands. What God requires on our part, however, is not an attempt at earning salvation but an ongoing effort to love God with all our heart and soul and mind and to love our neighbors as ourselves. We need humility and desire to work for the well-being of one another, which can be found only in community.

One place to begin this practice of humility and deepen the sense of community is the church. In the first chapter of his letter to the church, James identifies his concern with the wealthy, be it clergy or citizens, and then clearly develops his thoughts further in the second chapter:

> My brothers and sisters, do you with your acts of favoritism really believe in our glorious Lord Jesus Christ? For if a person with gold rings and fine clothes comes into your assembly, and if a poor person in dirty clothes also comes in, and if you take notice of the one wearing fine clothes and say, "Have a seat here, please," while to the one who is poor you say, "Stand there," or, "Sit at my feet," have you not made distinctions among yourselves, and become judges with evil thoughts? (James 2:1-4)

The show of favoritism or partiality was a concern for James and also an issue today. Research on this younger generation who consider themselves outside the church shows, "*84 percent* say they personally know at least one committed Christian. Yet just *15 percent* thought the lifestyles of those Christ followers were significantly different from the norm."[3] In other words, for those outside the church, the practice of being a Christian doesn't seem to make a difference. The next generation sees actions, both transparent and authentic, as important. This catches their attention.

For the Christian, the measuring stick for evaluating our lifestyle is nailed on the cross. We seek forgiveness regularly. We confess daily. Rich or poor, young or old, we live with humility. Humility does not mean we grovel and act as doormats to the world. It does mean we show no partiality. In heaven, wealth will not matter—nor will the color of our skin or our age or any of our trophies. As we pray for God's will to be done on earth as in heaven, it surely means we start now by showing no partiality.

Such a practice begins with humility, which bears all things, believes all things, hopes all things. A requirement for love is humility, which is patient and kind. We find it hard to imagine a person capable of love while arrogant or filled with pride. Think for a moment of the Pharisees, who were self-righteous and so very holy. Love does not seem to be evident in their circle, only anger, judgment, and a little gossip. Clearly, Jesus expects the church to carry the cross of humility, and in the process, not to lose our lives but find them.

I remember having the good fortune of going on a pilgrimage to Israel. Included in our visit was the Church of the Nativity, the holy site where Jesus was born in Bethlehem. As we entered the church, the only door was a small opening on one side. We had to bend down, kneel, and finally crawl to enter the church. The door was built small to prevent the horses and carts of looters from entering. Today, we refer to it only as "the door to humility." It reminds us that God expressed humility in coming to us in a manger and in the form of a baby. As we stoop and crawl to enter the church, our bodies recognize the change taking place. We kneel in all humility before the King of kings.

Jesus is the gate with James the pillar. The church contains the door of humility with no partiality, only love. As we get up off our knees, we realize we are not alone. We have stood the test. With all the saints, there awaits us, in all humility, the crown of life. James, in his letter, now turns our attention to move from favoritism to the joy of a faith community in heaven just as it is on earth.

CHAPTER SUMMARY

- James calls the church to show no partiality. When favoritism is shown to the rich, the church is in danger of seeking mammon and not the kingdom of God.
- Acquiring wealth and treasures on earth is limited by time and mortality. The rich will disappear like a

flower in the field. Death offers no material wealth. The danger comes with our desire by possessing treasures on earth, we can become possessed.

- Treasures in heaven begin with seeking first the kingdom of God. Treasures are found in our relationship with God in Christ who is safe in our heart. James and Jesus both speak to the relationship between heaven and the heart.
- "Resilient Disciples" want others to see Jesus reflected by their words and actions. They are mission oriented and not the church tomorrow, but today.
- Jesus is "the gate" as James is "the pillar." They provide the necessary space and place for the church to gather by entering through the door to humility. Humility is a requirement for love, and it is good for the soul and the church.

A Spiritual Exercise:

Who Owns Your Heart?

- Humility does not mean you do not matter, or that you are a nobody. It does have something to do with self-denial and recognizing that you are not the center of the universe—because we know who is. It also is the way to pick up your cross and follow Jesus. It is countercultural. How does your church develop younger leaders?
- The next generation wants others to see Jesus reflected in their words and actions. As a mentor, is there a way you can meet with younger adults and ask them in what ways were they intentional or conscious of re-presenting Jesus in the past twenty-four hours, or this past week, or month? Was this something others noticed? Did it merit discussion?
- Participating in a mission sounds like it requires time, fund raising, travel, planning, and results. In a countercultural mission the resilient disciple considers

it not nearly as extensive or foreboding. The action they take can be as simple as a tweet or text or maybe a cup of coffee. Perhaps a mission includes a simple pat on the back or word of encouragement. Their goal is to follow Jesus, sometimes catching people. Mission is a matter of the heart. Ask the young adults, who owns their heart?

- As a mentor share your thoughts about who owns *your* heart. Talk about favoritism, partiality, privilege and what you have seen, experienced, or learned in church and in your life. Ask your disciples, what might it take to show no partiality? What would be the risk, the cost, or the benefit if you were not the reference point, or what if the world did not revolve around you?

CHAPTER 8

ENCOURAGEMENT

"RECEIVE THE CROWN OF LIFE"

(JAMES 1:12)

My wife has a habit, or better yet, a spiritual practice, where she visits with people in the parish on Sunday afternoon. Whether birthdays, baptisms, or the grief over the loss of a loved one, she finds a way to simply poke her head in the door. Often, she will take flowers from church or a cake or dinner she cooked the night before, and with that, the visit begins. As the minister who usually stays up late Saturday night and gets up early Sunday morning, I'm always grateful to have the time alone in a quiet house for an afternoon nap. When she returns, I hear the stories of the people she visits and the conversations that take place, and I become profoundly aware—and just a tinge jealous—that although I preach a good game about community, she lives it.

When I asked her one evening why she made such an effort on a Sunday afternoon to visit, she said it reminds her of childhood and her mother. Every Sunday after church, they would visit people from the congregation. Rather than a chore, they thought of it as simply a way of keeping in touch. Her use of the word "touch" says it all.

Our contemporary culture seems so out of touch. We create social isolation by the way we organize family activities around sports, clubs, malls, restaurants, and social media. Rather than connect us at the end of the day, these pursuits make us feel disconnected. Instead of being in touch, we feel detached. Social scientists refer to the change taking place as "tribal" and like-minded, as compared to engagement and sharing stories, or simply catching up with neighbors and sincerely caring for one another. We tend further toward isolation.

Increased isolation breeds loneliness. Those paying attention to the statistical impact of the COVID-19 pandemic see not only the physical illness this virus has caused but the multifaceted complications, including an epidemic of loneliness—especially for elderly adults. When these elders were surveyed, "66 percent say their anxiety levels have increased,"[1] adding another dimension to their loneliness.

The obvious reason for concern is anxiety leads to stress, and with stress comes anger. Unresolved and unchecked due to isolation, anger can damage us both internally and externally. Sufferers may turn to addictions as a means of medicating their problems or develop patterns of self-destructive abuse, or even violence towards another. Focusing on healthy social relationships and the importance of community engagement are compromised by the data pouring in daily as we seek protection from the virus. Community life and the church, with regard to its corporate worship in particular, have been challenged during the pandemic. We see a growing need for a sense of belonging and a desire for family and friends. A vibrant faith community becomes an antidote, not necessarily to the spread of a virus, but to the epidemic of loneliness and the need for keeping in touch.

THE COMMUNITY OF JAMES

It is difficult to describe with absolute certainty what the early church communities were like in Jerusalem,

Rome, Antioch, or many of the cities identified by Paul in his missionary journeys. Nonetheless, we can conclude the first century was not for the fainthearted. Granted, as today's tourists walk along the paved marble street of Ephesus leading to the ancient ruins of the grand library, it is easy to imagine a life of gentility and pleasure. With beautiful temples, stadiums, and even running public toilets, it doesn't take much to picture Paul converting the masses like a modern-day Billy Graham. History, however, can quickly become romanticized and reduced to nothing more than a walk down the path of sentimentality.

The bleak reality was hunger, filth, violence, and overpopulation in many cities made epidemics acute and death ever present. Fear, disorder, and riots could erupt within the unbearable stench coming with warm weather and large public gatherings. Life in the first century was not pleasant. Viral epidemics led to chronic health conditions which further exacerbated high mortality rates and shortened life expectancy. It was not a question of poor hygiene—people simply had no soap or clean water. Again, we are talking about the larger cities. The notion of a community life that offered a sense of belonging and a place for friends and family where traditions were passed from generation to generation seemed hopelessly removed. With urban disarray and social disorder, alienation and loneliness comprised just one more threat in the long list of health concerns and overall well-being.

Within this context, the Christian faith community begins, and James brings a powerful witness to "stand"— not alone—but with the community of saints. The idea of standing together in the midst of dread, despair, and death offers a sign of strength and courage the Christian faith witnesses. Instead of anonymity, the church offers an identity as the body of Christ and a community of faith. Together the church community provides courage to take a stand and bear witness to the light and an abundant life, a life with God that is never ending. The early church presents both a compelling vision and an invitation to somehow, and in some way, make a difference to a world that is known only for indifference and darkness.

Rodney Stark, in his book on *The Rise of Christianity*, concludes:

> Christianity revitalized life in Greco-Roman cities by providing new norms and new kinds of social relationships able to cope with many urgent urban problems. To cities filled with the homeless and impoverished, Christianity offered charity as well as hope. To cities filled with newcomers and strangers, Christianity offered an immediate basis for attachments. To cities filled with orphans and widows, Christianity provided a new and expanded sense of family. To cities torn by violent ethnic strife, Christianity offered a new basis for social solidarity. And to cities faced with epidemics, fires, and earthquakes, Christianity offered effective nursing services.[2]

The church community was on a mission, not necessarily to become the number one religion nor the biggest and best of churches but simply to offer specific and effective help to those in need. The parable Jesus told of the good Samaritan reminded his listeners of the countercultural mission required for these early Christians. When giving aid, they would do it with no strings attached. People giving and receiving help need not be like-minded or have similar beliefs. It was not necessary to judge when offering assistance.

What we learn from the Samaritan is he simply gave what he could give and do what he could do, which began with first helping the bloodied and nearly dead man out of the ditch. He also poured oil on and bound up his wounds, and then put him on his donkey and took him to a nearby inn. From there, the Samaritan handed him off to an innkeeper with a few coins and the request to continue the help and service. That is the story. It clearly speaks to the Millennial and Gen Z Christians today. Like the Samaritan, they are responding to the need that is right before them. For they navigate a road encountering countless friends, associates, and strangers who are left in this proverbial ditch.

CHILDREN OF LIGHT

Barna Research identifies one of the most important practices the church can provide is by encouraging young Christians to engage in God's mission. That way, we support them in living a life of significance that helps others. Matching the gifts and skills of a young adult with a mission to serve taps into the longings we all have and makes and restores a better world. Results matter. So, too, does personalizing the mission. Exactly what that mission will be and where it can be found is often as close as a beaten man in the ditch— or a friend in recovery. And Barna cites the most important virtue we, the church, provide is courage.

> Acknowledging our fear and trusting God in spite of it are job one. Courage helps to empower our definition of discipleship: to develop Jesus followers who are resiliently faithful in the face of cultural coercion and who live a vibrant life in the Spirit. Without courage, we won't stand up for the right things at the right time. Seven out of ten say their churches help them to find "courage to live my faith in public" and "wisdom for how to live faithfully in a secular world.[3]

Seven out of ten is an extraordinary percentage, yet this statistic need not surprise us. Courage for the Christian does not just happen. It arrives as character trait, a virtue, a gift that comes to us from God's kingdom, and we must claim it. The faith community accepts this gift of courage and teaches it, reinforces it through Jesus who reminds us of persecution and troubles in the world, "But take courage; I have conquered the world" (John 16:33).

In his letter to the church, James speaks clearly about our ability to serve, to make a difference, to sustain a well-lived life since it all originates from "the Father of light." (James 1:17) No doubt, this understanding originates from the wisdom teaching of Jesus who, in the Sermon on the Mount, tells the pure in heart, the merciful, the persecuted, the common people who rely upon God in this faith community that they are not only blessed but they are "the light of the world." He further instructs them to let their "light shine before others, so that that may see your good works and give glory to your Father in heaven "(Matthew 5: 14, 16). This is our mission regardless of the darkness that may surround us. Be of courage.

BE THE LIGHT

Such an understanding of courage reflects the brightness found in grace, or as Paul refers to us—"children of light" (I Thessalonians 5:5). This clarity reminds us our life in Christ is found and revealed when we lack nothing, pray in faith, show no partiality, and no longer are in the dark. People in the dark are filled with fear. Yet God's glory brings forth courage, strength, and grace to break through and rise above fear so that we may live a life with God whose abundance satisfies our yearnings. Light, courage, and life team up and work together. From the beginning of creation when God first brought life into being, we hear these words of origin: "Let there be light" (Genesis 1:3). This same brilliance is incarnate, incorporated into the truth of Christ, as his "light shines in the darkness, and the darkness did not overcome it." (John 1:5).

We stand as children of the light and with courage serve in mission by making a difference to those in need and to the world around us. This call for mission is the same as it has always been when Jesus first commissioned us by serving him "to the end of the age" (Matthew 28:20). We never stop bringing the light and the knowledge of where we find light. We find God's glory filled with life, and this brightness that not only shines in the darkness but exposes the truth. Bearing witness to the truth—taking a stand—is not easy. It brings us to the test. It requires courage. So, hold closely the word of Jesus who says, "Take courage, I have conquered the world" (John 16:33)

STAND THE TEST

As we engage in mission, James reminds us to "stand the test" (1:12). The test is unlike any other. This test is administered by the devil. From the Greek, we find the word "test" can also be translated as "temptation" or "trial." In fact, different readings of the Lord's Prayer appear in the Episcopal *Book of Common Prayer,* with the traditional wording, "and lead us not into temptation" and the more contemporary reading, "Save us from the time of trial."[4]

We make this distinction because the Greek word *peirazō* has different shades of meaning that alter not only the translation but the theology, which can misrepresent God as the tempter. James clarifies this point when writing about the test or temptation: "No one, when tempted, should say, 'I am being tempted by God'; for God cannot be tempted by evil and he himself tempts no one." (James 1:13).

James follows this understanding with the powerful chain reaction that when "desire has conceived, it gives birth to sin, and that sin, when it is fully grown, gives birth to death." (James 1:15) Look out for the test, the temptation, or the trial and be assured the cross is an ever-present reminder of our salvation and deliverance from this spiritual battle of good and evil.

As an example, the story of Jesus in the wilderness for forty days and forty nights warns us how serious the test can be and what is required to stand, especially when standing up to evil, darkness, and the devil. During this time, Satan tempts—or tests—Jesus to turn stones into bread, to leap from the temple, or ultimately, to worship the devil.

This test is no exam for a grade. Rather this is a test for the life that Jesus would carry with him all the way to the cross. To each temptation in the desert as well as on the cross, Jesus relies upon the strength and courage he finds in Scripture, the Word of God. Each temptation is the devil's skill at deception or as the Bible reveals, the devil is the "deceiver of the whole world" (Revelation 12: 9). Such a cosmic test takes place in the desert for forty days and again in the garden of Gethsemane coaxing Jesus to surrender. Yet, "the desire of the flesh, the desire of the eyes, the pride in riches does not come from the Father" (I John 2:16).

This is not a story from long ago, but it is our reality today. Standing for goodness in the world inevitably reveals evil lurking around the corner. If we stand with the saints for the truth, we must look out for lies and dishonesty to attack. As we stand for peace, we also face the prospect of war, hate, and unrest. Psychology and modern-day social sciences try and explain, but the idea of spiritual warfare speaks directly to the misplaced desires and darkness that keep the pot boiling, with the devil using the world as a personal playground.

Since that is the case, then the battle before us is surely a spiritual one, and the witness of James speaks clearly and resonates with the church today and a new generation like never before.

Barna research addresses this strong sense of mission with somewhat startling results, again as we found in 90 percent of the resilient disciples who "want others to see Jesus reflected in me through my words and actions."[5] This is impressive not simply by the high percentage but because these young adults assume Jesus is not for Sunday morning only. He dwells very much with them at work, at home, and at play. It is who they are. In fact, Jesus chooses them for this time and place to do the mission and hard work of reconciling and restoring the world to God.

James echoes this sentiment because of the victory on the cross being tested by writing, "My brothers and sisters, whenever you face trials of any kind, consider it nothing but joy" (James 1: 2).

I AM THE LIGHT OF THE WORLD

We experience joy while living in and trusting God. This joy is made manifest especially to a church on mission. These times call for compassion and not only understanding but standing. Taking a stand for our brothers and sisters does not divide or polarize, but it does mean we stand to help. Never alone, we are surrounded by a great cloud of witnesses who have gone before us. The crown of life awaits us and signifies the kingdom of God, referring to life with God that is a reflection of the light. In fact, Scripture tells us, "God is light and in him there is no darkness at all." (I John 1:5)

John's gospel further tells us this light that came into the world shines in the darkness and darkness has not overcome it. Darkness makes it hard to see, but like the four horsemen of the apocalypse, we do see the effects of the demonic in the dread, despair, deception, and death. These horsemen team up in the dark to extinguish the light of the world.

Yet, Jesus says, "I am the light of the world." (John 8:12) This is another one of the I AM sayings the early church held onto because their times were dark. By holding onto this light, they found their mission and the daily tests they faced made easier because they could meet them with joy. Joy enters our world by living in and trusting God and rejecting sin. Jesus brings this to light with the woman caught in adultery.

The Pharisees bring the woman before Jesus. They present their case and the law of Moses, which clearly states she should be stoned to death. To Jesus, they simply ask, "Now what do you say?" (John 8:5). This, of course, is a test and after further questioning by the Pharisees, Jesus says to them, "Let anyone among you who is without sin be the first to throw a stone at her." (John 8:7) The Pharisees leave this scene of humiliation one by one, while Jesus stays with the women and assures her she will not be condemned. Later, he tells the Pharisees "I am the light of the world" (John 8:12). The light of Jesus brings life not death. It brings forgiveness and not condemnation. The sheer brightness helps us recognize the presence of God and the absence of sin. It is not hidden under a bushel. It reveals God.

The crown of life is not given only when we die. It is not like a diploma that is held out when we graduate. This crown is not something we earn but rather it is designed to fit and be worn in this life as we experience the reality of becoming children of the light. We have been tested, and we stand not with the darkness of sin but with the light of God. The light surrounds the company of saints who form a community of faith that is recognized for bringing heaven to earth and earth to heaven. The gift of generosity appears in this light that comes from above and shines with brightness as it further reflects the good works as we give glory to God. So, we turn next to generosity.

CHAPTER SUMMARY

- For a culture that breeds isolation and alienation James reminds us of the importance found in a vibrant faith community and the fact we're not standing alone.
- Together the church community is by design the body of Christ and provides courage to stand and bear witness to an abundant life, a life with God that is eternal and never ending.
- As we engage in mission, James reminds us to "stand the test" (1:12). The test is unlike any other. It is

ultimately a trial that brings us up against the darkness of the world, evil, and the demonic. By facing such trials, and as a result of the victory in the Cross, we join James by counting it "nothing but joy." (James 1:2)

- In facing the trials before us while on mission, we will receive the "crown of life" —a reflection of the kingdom work here on earth just as it is in heaven. This reflection is of Jesus, who is "the light of the world."

A SPIRITUAL EXERCISE: SERVING OTHERS

HOW CAN I MAKE A DIFFERENCE?

Courage is among the most important virtues we can cultivate. Acknowledging our fear and trusting God in spite of it are job one. Courage helps to empower our definition of discipleship: to develop Jesus followers who are resiliently faithful in the face of cultural coercion and who live a vibrant life in the Spirit.[6]

- The importance of community advances the mission where we stand together as the body of Christ and offer help and hope to those in need. As mentors, meet with young adults who want your wisdom and to experience of ways the church has given you courage to make a difference. Do you have examples of how your faith has made a difference in the lives of others? How might you respond?
- Preparing for mission may include simply a cup of coffee or a lunch with a fellow coworker. The small tasks may lead to something much greater. They are like a mustard seed. In time, the kingdom of God grows. Young people today are navigating an ever-changing landscape when it comes to church and spirituality, and there is a diversity of opinion. Include a time where you can meet and reflect together on various difficult conversations they have had with others regarding the church and their faith.

- Young adults learn from differences of opinion. They do not want to exclude but include. They do not want to judge but accept. Their culture is pluralistic. How to identify those who are in need and want our help is tricky. Working together in shared mission begins with you as mentor. Consider your gifts, skills, and competencies, and how you might make a difference in the world today.

CHAPTER 9

GENEROSITY

"EVERY PERFECT GIFT, IS FROM ABOVE"

(JAMES 1:17)

We have discussed to this point how James provided leadership for the early church in Jerusalem and was considered by some to be the first bishop. Moreover, in one of his earliest letters, Paul identifies James to the Galatians as the one who welcomes Paul and Peter for a visit in Jerusalem. Scholars estimate this visit took place somewhere before 36 AD,[1] which sets the context of the meeting shortly after the resurrection appearances of Jesus. Herein lies the story of the Christian church from the earliest days of formation, and it takes our breath away to imagine the conversation taking place among Paul, Peter, and James. Far from having an ordinary church meeting, these three men assemble under one roof to discuss their firsthand experiences personalized around the risen Jesus. The impact this new life in Christ offers through the resurrection and the power of the Holy Spirit can be found in each man's unique story and witness.

Paul no doubt speaks of his remarkable Damascus Road experience (Acts 9:1-9). The physicality of his conversion from being blinded by the light to seeing in a new way after his three years in Arabia reflects his profound renewal.

Included in his story is the movement from persecutor of Christians to following Jesus as Lord and Savior, which is not only well documented in his letters, but for Paul became a sign of both the grace and the authority given to him.

Fresh in Peter's mind was no doubt his living encounter with Jesus on the shore of the Sea of Galilee (John 21). Recall Peter initially planned to go back fishing and hold onto the past, especially after the horror of the crucifixion. By living in a time forgotten, Peter could repress the pain and grief over his gut-wrenching denials to the girl servant by the charcoal fire rather than facing Jesus upon the cross. From the depths of that despair, with dawn breaking, Peter hears the voice he will never forget, "Have you not caught anything?" He swims to the shore and there sits Jesus preparing breakfast. Three times, Peter confesses his love for the risen Lord only to hear Jesus say, "feed my sheep."

Everyone has a story to tell. James is no different. He, too, experienced his own personal revelation when the risen Lord appeared to him. Even if not documented, we are aware that in place of anger or revenge following the crucifixion of his brother, James speaks of God only as "good" and "perfect." In fact, Jesus is the good and perfect gift. James understands now, in light of the resurrection, that Jesus truly is the light of the world who is given to us from God, "the father of lights" (James 1:17). This light is the same power and energy with us from the beginning of creation and now extended to us in the new creation of life in Christ and in his kingdom. These attributes of God's benevolence, goodness, and love are constant and in never-ending supply, especially now as James stands in the glow of Jesus's resurrection. Peter and Paul share the same brightness as they gather together in counsel and light up the room.

God's light has power to transform and change, as Paul categorizes his reputation in this meeting as, "the one who formerly was persecuting is now proclaiming the faith he once tried to destroy" (Galatians 1:23). Fourteen years later, Paul refers to his meeting in Jerusalem with the early church leaders and again, names James and Peter, whom Paul calls "acknowledged pillars" (Galatians 2:10). The focus of the second meeting in Jerusalem is different from the first because Paul seeks approval for his missionary journey with Barnabas and a blessing of encouragement to expand the gospel from Jerusalem to all nations. The time has come, and Paul is ready to go and light up not simply a room but now to light up the world. The power and energy in these meetings reflect the radiance of the Holy Spirit, the risen Lord, and the Father of lights. And this same power and energy forms and shapes the character of the church, the *ecclēsia*. The gathering of those who today break bread in the presence of Christ, the incarnate light, participate in the reality found in the kingdom of God shining on earth, as it is in heaven.

Within this remarkable context and setting, the Christian church, the community of faith, was on a trajectory of unimaginable development and growth, where James asks only one thing of Paul and Barnabas: "remember the poor" (Galatians 2:10). The poor rely solely upon God with every good and perfect gift that blesses them as children of God. In remembering the poor, the church is generous. James instills this understanding of generosity as more than an ethical act within Paul's mission. Generosity is now a character trait for the church.

GENEROSITY

For James, generosity clearly entails more than giving money to those in need. He does not simply mean for those who have to give to those who have not. Generosity is spiritual in nature, more than a physical, one-way material exchange. Giving, sharing, helping are forms of hope, a way of extending ourselves through God's mercy for one another.

Generosity is also about change and transformation in both the person who gives and who receives. Generosity is a form of love. In fact, it may be considered love in action. As James calls it, "doing the word" is a good deed, a good gift, all as a result of a good God.

The church today teaches this understanding of generosity. An open hand, an extended hand, is far different from a closed fist. We find it more blessed to give because God gives. In fact, all good gifts are "from above" (James 1:17). As with the power of light, giving is an attribute of God. God invites the church to tap into this source of divine life through generosity. With God there is always enough, there is more than enough, there is an abundance—providing there is generosity.

In our day, as we well know, not everyone has enough. Obviously, in poor, third world countries, we are aware of the need for more—more clean water, more food, more shelter. The list seems endless. Yet even in the first world countries, with ways of exchanging goods and making payments to others, many still think about needing more. More income and more purchasing power are needed with automatic transfers in our credit card economy that seems sufficient until the end of a month when more is required. We tell ourselves the stock market prices are only as good as the paper they are printed on, so more stock. Our current portfolio is never enough. The cry for "more" often sounds louder and clashes with the words of James to "remember the poor."

The thirst for "more" becomes an obsession, and with it, we rationalize that generosity can be postponed or becomes expendable. We reassure ourselves, thinking someday, we will have enough, and then we will be generous. Whether or not that day arrives, we tighten our belt and wonder if there is enough. Of course, you know and I know, some will never find enough. Even some billionaires want more.

James, however, knows generosity is a gift from God. Money is not the problem. The problem is our desires. Scripture reminds us of this reality, "the love of money is a root of all kinds of evil, and in their eagerness to be rich some have wandered away from the faith" (I Timothy 6:10). Two key words are "love" and "eagerness." Obviously, our love for God has been misplaced and is replaced only by the love of money and what we think money can do. As a result, we lose the love of generosity. Our eagerness for more refers to our will, which means our intentions are misdirected. So again, our acts of generosity and God's will is not done on earth as it is in heaven. This struggle for "enough" while far from simple, involves a fundamental spiritual concern. When we "wander away from the faith" as Scripture warns, we wander away from our life with God, and we "like a flower will wither away." (James 1:11)

James tells us, especially as we struggle over needs or wants, "If any of you is lacking in wisdom, ask God, who gives to all generously and ungrudgingly, and it will be given you" (James 1: 5). God gives. God is generous. Generosity lies at the heart of God's character and reflects the image of God. By design, generosity then forms the Christian character.

GOD LOVES A CHEERFUL GIVER

When we hear, "God loves a cheerful giver" (2 Corinthians 9:7) in church, we either reach into our pockets or hold on to our wallets, because we know the pastor is requesting funds. As a clergyman, I relied on this verse. Like any verse in Scripture, it can be taken out of context and used—or misused—to support the need to give, whether cheerfully or not. In fact, periodically, some disgruntled parishioner would ask me, "How do you know God loves a cheerful giver?" My fallback response early in the ministry was to shield myself from the criticism behind the question and simply point out the verse as it is written by Paul in the Bible. That seemed to help some.

Interestingly, the more I reflected upon and critiqued this verse, the more I matured with respect to money and grew in giving. I simply encouraged parishioners to think about our image of God as a cheerful giver. I gave sermons and taught classes and walked and talked about this attribute of God and more importantly, our fundamental relationship and primary image of God. The message of thinking about God as a cheerful giver and not as a grumpy old man who sits on his throne and throws lightning bolts at us not only seemed to work, but it struck a deeper chord with our need for satisfaction. Generosity satisfies. Greed does not.

To have a healthy image of God, we rely on the authority of Scripture because it reveals over time an understanding of our Christian character formation and how the practice of generosity shapes our identity. We are generous not simply because we donate here and there, but because God expects us to. God loves cheerful givers because, yes, God is a cheerful giver, and God makes us in the image of himself. This does not mean we look like God, but we reflect God's character in our lives. This understanding of being made in God's image first appears in the story of creation where God forms us and creates us as stewards of creation. Generosity flows out of the image of God, out of our character as stewards who manage, and all that God has given us. A good steward is generous and blessed.

This understanding of generosity as a characteristic trait of God, and a spiritual attribute of our lives that reflects the image of God, carries us beyond money and on into the deeper awareness of our identity. Acting miserly over our handling of money speaks directly to our personality. The money is important. But the person is more important.

Paul writes, "If I give away all my possessions, and if I hand over my body so that I may boast, but do not have love, I gain nothing" (1 Corinthians 13:3). Even if we don't attach strings to our giving, others can detect a spirit by our attitude and character as to how we assess the worth and value of ourselves. We may place a high value on the act of generosity, but that does not mean we think highly of ourselves. Our names may be on plaques, windows, and buildings, but our name does not matter. What counts far more is how we value and respect ourselves in light of God's creation.

One other thought with respect to generosity: often, we are taught generosity is about money. "Made in God's image" is not about what we look like or how we appear, but it simply means we are stewards of our resources and give cheerfully, as God gives cheerfully. We may have lots of money, but then again, we may not. What we all have within is the thumbprint of God upon our souls, who has created us with an image that imagines and fills our imagination with countless opportunities to give and contribute in making the world more creative as it was in the creation. We all have gifts, talents, and competencies that others can benefit from.

When we have electrical problems, as an example, I call Terry, my friend who is an electrician to ask for help. Without Terry, things could really go badly around our house. (They could go bad for me as well.) I know danger, and I know my limits. In Terry, God has blessed me with a friend who possesses skills I lack.

A cynic might consider Terry's work as an electrician simply a job. Nothing more. Nothing less. For me, I value Terry and value his time and his explanations and appreciate the pride that goes into his work. When he helps me out, I remember the hymn, "Count Your Blessings." I've learned from Terry that generous people "share their blessings one by one." They make the world better.

When I learned to think of not only counting blessings but sharing blessing as a form of generosity, it seemed to flip the switch in the parish where I served. The church was filled with blessings. One by one, I count them.

HONORING GOD

The Barna Group found yet another astonishing statistic in their research of resilient disciples, one pertaining to the way they integrate their work with their faith. While generosity is important to them, debt places higher in their list of concerns. Accumulated indebtedness, from credit cards to student loans or financial pressure from falling behind on car payments or rent, adds up to make money a huge problem for young adults. But as great an obstacle as personal debt poses for anyone at any age, the resilient disciple's desire to honor God with unique talents and gifts stands as one of the highest affirmations and characteristics for this next generation. They will give generously of their time and talent. They bring focus to an understanding of generosity that includes compassion and making a tangible difference—both of which do not necessarily require money. Watch this understanding unfold as it pushes the button for generosity in a remarkable statistic.

Ninety-four percent, or nine out of ten, say "I want to use my unique talents and gifts to honor God."[2] Generosity as a form of self-giving reveals a love that abounds in a generation standing in line ready to give. This is terribly exciting. No one is saying money does not count. Having money and giving money simply do not register as a sole motivator for generosity.

This brings us back to sharing blessings. Scripture tells us compassion is yet another attribute or characteristic of God, and this same trait overflows through the teachings, parables, and actions of Jesus where time and again "when he saw the crowds, he had compassion for them" (Matthew 9:36). Compassion is a blessing. We see it when Jesus fed the five thousand, Then, again, we are reminded of the return of the prodigal son and how the father received him home with open arms and "was filled with compassion" (Luke 15:20). Of course, the same holds true with the Good Samaritan.

Compassion demonstrates a deep love for people, and we find tenderness, kindness, and mercy closely following compassion. It need not surprise us when we look simply at the word compassion, and we find compass imbedded within it. A compass helps us describe compassion as we allow our hearts to direct and guide us. Compassion is not necessarily our "North Star" but rather exhibits a form of love that is grounded and radiates heaven on earth. This kind of love requires hard work.

Just as the word "compass" is found in compassion, so its Latin root word, *pati* translates as "suffer." Compassion describes one who literally is willing to "suffer with." We identify with another's suffering and help others with their suffering, and passion then governs what we do.

When we think of the next generation, this discussion resonates deeply with a desire to honor God, not out of obligation or duty but because passion calls. The idea of being able to help another and make a personal difference provides a key motivation. My wife and I are most aware of this respect for compassion and the importance found in sharing blessings at a personal level through the generosity of our adult sons and daughters-in-law. They have taught us when we give of ourselves, we enrich life for others. Living, in other words, has to do with giving, and this form of living never ends.

I AM THE VINE

Our eldest son, Ben, was diagnosed at age thirty-five with stage-4 metastatic colon cancer. To say the diagnosis came as a shock doesn't come close to describing our feelings. Words cannot express adequately the suffering and the illness and eventually the death that accompanies such a diagnosis and experience. I can imagine no worse pain than that of parents burying their child. But I am also well aware of the impact the loss makes on the entire family system. The brothers were devastated, and the daughters-in-law and grandchildren also experienced their own unique grief as they extended comfort one to another. The experience severely impacted everyone who knew and loved Ben.

The importance of family and the strength of family carried my wife and me, to be sure. But I bring this personal story to the surface because I noticed how my sons and daughters-in-law wanted to do something. They did not want death to have the last word. Together, they desired to honor Ben's legacy and ultimately honor God. They joined efforts and provided leadership with the Colon Cancer Prevention Project in Kentucky. This project brings awareness and educational programs for health care providers and social workers who partner with like-minded organizations to remove barriers and encourage screening throughout Kentucky. Through the generosity of this remarkable project, screening rates have gone from 33 percent in 2004 to more than 70 percent today. This means one less person is dying each day from colon cancer in Kentucky. Again, I share this story because it reinforces the higher calling young people have to make a difference in a way that honors God and restores the health and well-being of those in need. Compassion motivates generosity and honors God, which in turn, bears fruit.

The early church was aware of this imagery of bearing fruit that originates with the desire of honoring God. James writes in his letter, "Wisdom from above is first pure, then peaceable, gentle, willing to yield, full of mercy and good fruits, without a trace of partiality or hypocrisy" (James 3:17).

In the context of upper room, on the night before Jesus dies, John writes of Jesus strengthening his disciples with the claim, "I am the true vine, and my Father is the vine grower. My father is glorified, that you bear much fruit" (John 15:1,8). This motif is a powerful reminder found in the interrelationship between the vine, the vine grower, and the fruit. It speaks to our calling of generosity motivated by compassion, which, in honoring God, bears fruit. This fruit is ripe and made available to the community of faith. We find such fruit in the work of restoration specifically in a church whose willingness to witness appears when they are "slow to speak and slow to anger" (James 1:19). James knows and bears witness to the fact that anger brings heat but at times can become too hot. Generosity, however, warms us to be sure, and when we hold generosity out—like iron—it can be forged into a witness of effective leadership for the community. Such leadership is resilient, and it is to these resilient disciples we turn our attention to the importance and promise found in the church witness.

CHAPTER SUMMARY

- In remembering the poor, the church learns the importance of generosity. This value of generosity is more than an idea or a kind gesture. James instills within Paul's mission an attribute for the church and a deeper understanding of being in communion with God and our neighbor.
- Generosity is spiritual in nature, more than a physical, one-way material exchange. It is also about change and transformation for both the person who gives and the one who receives. Generosity is a form of love. James calls it "doing the word."
- God loves cheerful givers because, yes, God is a cheerful giver, and God makes us in the image of himself.
- Jesus says, "I am the vine" (John 15:1). This imagery cultivates generosity when motivated by compassion and honors God by bearing fruit.

A Spiritual Exercise:
Intergenerational Relationships

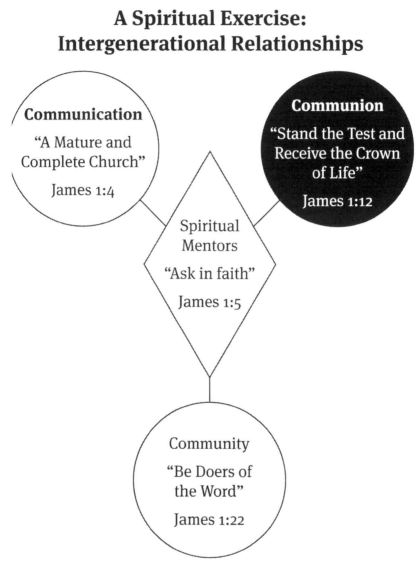

According to Barna Research, "There are two signposts that can lead toward meaningful, intergenerational relationships; one is **aspirational,** and the other is **reality-based**."[3] (Emphasis added) Aspirational represents the best in, or the ideal of, the church. Reality-based is ordinary, everyday church—warts and all.

Reflect as a mentor and mentee on the church attributes in Part Two and identify which characteristics most strongly bring you into communion with different generations. Then select the attribute you think requires greater attention.

PART THREE

THE CHURCH WITNESS: COMMUNITY

Community is the context for the growth of convictions and character. What we believe about life and the world becomes plausible as we see it lived out all around us. This is not an abstraction, though. Its reality is seen in time and space, in the histories and circumstances of real people living real lives.

—**Steven Garber**, *The Fabric of Faithfulness*[1]

Living in the tension between these—the great good of Christian community and the lived reality of its imperfections—is hard, soul-crafting work. And because of the ascendant cultural forces of isolation and loneliness, this work is more needed than ever.

—David Kinnaman & Mark Matlock, *Faith for Exiles*[2]

CHAPTER 10

LEADERSHIP

"BE QUICK TO LISTEN, SLOW TO SPEAK, SLOW TO ANGER" (JAMES 1:19)

Both the Holy Spirit and the firsthand witness to the resurrection of Jesus empowered the development of the Christian community. Church expansion, however, required leadership. Here again we turn our attention to James, the pillar and now the assumed leader in the Jerusalem church.

As the early church grew, a hotly contested debate ensued over teaching and conversion to Christianity. The matter of circumcision and dietary laws may seem far removed from our day and age, but the division revealed the deep question of Christian identity. The requirement for becoming a Christian was something new to consider, and the early basic beliefs of Christianity all set the foundation upon which the church would stand. Cohesion and agreement were necessary. Otherwise, schisms and false teachers would emerge and lead these young, impressionable Christians astray. This was a dangerous time that had the appearance of a crisis in the making as the fundamental law of Moses was now being challenged and "the apostles and the elders met together to consider this matter" (Acts 15:6). This generational gathering of church leaders, later referred to as the "Jerusalem Council" was recorded in Acts and further described by Paul in Galatians. It stands as the first apostolic council documented in Christian church history.

Theologians and historians alike still debate the events and the outcome of the council. The dynamics at work and the rift taking place among those gathered no doubt polarized and quickly divided those in attendance at the meeting. They seemed to find no middle ground. Into this cauldron of heated emotion and apparently raw conflict, James, Peter, Paul, and Barnabas entered. The controversial split over circumcision and the practice of dietary rules appeared as presenting issues, but beneath those concerns lay far deeper matters of Christian identity for both the Jew and the Gentile.

The council begins with agreeing God's judgment falls on all humankind in Israel and beyond. Everyone must repent, Jews and Gentiles alike. Only one God exists, and any other deities are false idols. The debate turned towards the Gentiles who were questioned for not living fully as Jews. Council members also raised issues over salvation and fellowship in the very kingdom of God, which the Messiah Jesus lived for and for which he died and rose again to reign. Much anger and disagreement followed. Paul is clearly on the side of welcoming righteous Gentiles. Peter stands his ground with those who maintain kosher purity and the difference in Jewish and Gentile table fellowship. Obviously, if Jews and Gentiles cannot eat together, then Peter considered worshipping together out of the question. In fact, according to Paul, the matter needed resolution.

In his letter to the Galatians, Paul makes public his conflict with Peter and others in the Jerusalem council, and he doesn't hide his very strident, personal disagreement by writing, "there are some who are confusing you and want to pervert the gospel of Christ and are turning to a different gospel" (Galatians 1:7). This different gospel—or perversion of the gospel—had previously created chaos in Antioch where "certain individuals came down from Judea and were teaching the brothers, "'Unless you are circumcised according to the custom of Moses, you cannot be saved'" (Acts 15:1). Herein lies the central question of salvation. As a result of the Jerusalem council, Paul writes to the Gentiles that the law is a custodian—in current jargon, nothing more than a babysitter. He emphasizes further we are not only set free from the bondage of sin and the law *through* faith in Christ, but we are saved by faith *in* Christ. Paul draws a dividing line.

We give attention to this disagreement not only because of its importance to the early church community but because the formation of Christian identity is an issue from generation to generation.

After everyone has spoken, James replies as the leader of the church who has the final word. Regarding this dispute, some may think James sidestepped the division with a "live and let live" compromise. Certainly, according to Paul's later writings, the tension was not alleviated. The factions remained. Yet what we find in the comments recorded by James are a clear recognition of his leadership and his understanding of being "quick to listen, slow to speak, slow to anger" (James 1:19). Read again his words,

> Therefore, I have reached the decision that we should not trouble those Gentiles who are turning to God, but we should write to them to abstain only from things polluted by idols and from fornication and from whatever has been strangled and from blood. For in every city, for generations past, Moses has had those who proclaim him, for he has been read aloud every sabbath in the synagogues. (Acts 15:19-21)

As mentioned previously, James at this time further extends the right hand of fellowship and "asked only one thing, that we remember the poor" (Galatians 2:10). With that, we begin to set this meeting within the context of our witness as the church community and contemplate the matter of Christian identity. The example James provides offers us several insights in leadership for spiritual mentors and the next generation worthy of our consideration today.

QUICK TO LISTEN

Listening is often taught these days as a skill. I guess it could be considered a skill. Personally, I side with someone like Dietrich Bonhoeffer who identified listening as an act of service. He wrote, "The first service that one owes to others in the fellowship consists in listening to them. Just as love to God begins with listening to His Word, so the beginning of love for the brethren is learning to listen to them."[1]

As a discipline, listening leads to virtues such as patience. In other words, listening is a good discipline. It also bodes well for leadership. When a leader listens, it demonstrates a mutual desire to learn, grow, and be part of the solution and not the problem, developing a sense of ownership for all involved. Listening doesn't mean you have nothing to say. Rather it demonstrates a need to find an answer together rather than again having the answer dictated from an authoritative source beyond question. Good listening naturally allows for good questions and represents freedom from expectations of having all the answers or being the smartest person in the room.

The person listening internalizes what is said by reflecting, ruminating, and discerning the images, ideas, and thoughts being articulated. We can appreciate listening as a creative, spiritual act, and thereby find ourselves close to the Creator (who is *the* listener), enabling us to develop an expectation that something will be created.

Well-known author and consultant in the area of leadership is Max DePree who writes "the first responsibility of a leader is to define reality."[2] Be assured, I discovered the service of listening the hard way. Like many pastors, I found myself in the midst of a multimillion-dollar capital campaign for a building program to expand our church facilities. The process did not happen in one day. What seemingly occurred overnight, however, was my awareness of the heavy weight placed on my shoulders as a result of leadership.

Early on in my ministry, I completed a three-year extension program in spiritual direction from the Shalem Institute in Washington DC. The program basically taught an extrovert like me to be quiet. It had a profound effect on me and opened me at many levels but particularly the desire to listen for God. Without going into great detail, I found joy reading Scripture through the *Lectio Divina* process and with it came a real interest in journaling like never before. Considerable time was spent as well at the nearby Abby of Gethsemane, where I underwent personal direction and learned to appreciate the contemplative side of my life. This wonderful spiritual movement taking place in my life provided me with a new insight to marriage and parenting. Life with four boys seemed challenging at times but nonetheless good. All was well, or so I thought.

Then one Sunday after church, my wife said to me, "You look so holy sitting up there at the altar. You have no idea what it is like in the pews." According to Max Depree, my wife was defining reality.

I heard her loud and clear. I began spending time on Sunday mornings looking around. Church consultants told me that in the first minute after getting out of a car, newcomers acquire a lasting first impression of the church. A crowded parking lot, no one to greet or welcome them, uncomfortable, overflowing seating capacity, bathrooms in need of attention, limited childcare and classroom space—all this adds up and makes for a poor impression. It became apparent something needed to be done.

Without going through all the drama of a building program and a capital campaign, it became obvious to me I didn't have the answer to our many problems. There was no quick fix. But through the grace of God, we began to organize "listening sessions" that allowed for parishioners to articulate their hopes and desires for the parish and community. This not only gave them ownership and a literal buy-in to the process but transformed the terrific burden that was on my shoulders into a new form of leadership. As I look back at this time, I can see by listening to one another, we were all in this together, and with the gift of a new day, we were ready to go. Listening is truly a form of service. Servant leadership by its nature includes a listening ear.

The Emotional Climate of the Church

Before going further on the connection found in listening and leadership, I trust you are not reading into this discussion that James was developing a corporate CEO résumé in the Jerusalem church. All too often, churches, regardless of denomination or size get swept into a business management mode. Of course, the church needs to remain mindful of certain business traits. Otherwise, it would have to close the doors. But some church leaders, by looking to other professions for the answer, overlook the simple but profound gift listening provides for the formation and the witness of a parish community.

James also includes in his advice that leaders are "slow to speak, slow to anger" (James 1:9). I'm not saying James wants leaders to be wallflowers or expects them to stay cool, calm, and collected at all times. Rather than targeting the leader's personality, James concentrates on the emotions and beliefs of the people he serves. He exhibits not a private, self-centered concern but an outward, other-person approach. In so doing, James brings to the surface a relevant topic for today that revolves around civility.

We all know about wedge issues. We are aware how quickly communication is manipulated, and messages are reduced to bullet points and the spinning of words is deceptive. The media keeps telling us we are divided and polarized as a country. Yet James advocates rather for compassion and empathy, which side-by-side, seem to go a long way in serving the next generation. Being nice, being civil, or simply listening, is not about conflict avoidance, or sugarcoating, or sweeping serious problems under the rug. A person of empathy and compassion is less concerned about winning and competing and more interested in serving and helping. The church community by design is not made to give trophies and ribbons but it is built to forge and strengthen relationships within us and around us and ultimately through our relationship with God. Compassion and empathy when extended fills the emotional climate of a church and appreciates and values other people as a gift or a blessing given to us by God and for a reason that is waiting to be discovered.

Barna Research finds churches that pay attention to meaningful relationships and help create strong relational networks also build resilient disciples. When interviewed, 83 percent of these resilient disciples said they had in church at least "one close friend I trust with my secrets."[3] That sounds simple. But according to Barna "relationships are meaningful when we are devoted to fellow believers we want to be around and become."[4] Such relationships are not easy to forge. But it can be done by paying attention to emotions. This is where judgment, stress, and anger can collide with the sensitivity of young adults. They don't expect conflict in church. They expect Christians to be loving—or at the least civil. This is a relevant concern for today, and no wonder. An offensive, rude, ill-mannered culture seems to have been unleashed and is lurking all around. Is the church different?

The desire to know the people around us makes the church different. We are not anonymous. The church is not a club where people pay their dues and have a right to complain. The church cares. Of course, in the best of families, as in the best of churches, conflict and disagreement surface. We witnessed this with James and in the Jerusalem Council. James teaches us to deal with conflict. He does not deny conflict but seeks to recognize the problem head on. According to Scripture, he doesn't exacerbate or worsen the situation. Instead, he is slow to speak, and we find no record of his anger as we see with others. He does not offend anyone. Nor did he appear as if he were placating. We learn from his leadership to respond in a thoughtful, proactive way so all who are in attendance find something they can agree upon— "only one thing, that we remember the poor"—which Paul goes on to write he is "eager to do." (Galatians 2:10).

INTERGENERATIONAL RELATIONSHIPS

This eagerness described by Paul provides insight into something of the emotional health at work in the church. What Paul demonstrates does not equate to a puppy wagging its tail and jumping up and down in anticipation of a treat, but rather it involves Paul's deep desire to serve and bear witness as a matter of the will, meaning he is intentional and eager to pass the Gospel truth from one generation to the next.

The leadership, then as now, in examining the emotional health within the church community, should be aware of meaningful relationships in the church and plan intergenerational relationships. This, again, provides a crucial role for spiritual mentors. Barna recognizes that 65 percent of resilient disciples "feel valued by the people in my life who are older than me."[5] Barna further presses these relationships to include "reciprocal mentoring" meaning the job of the mentor is not to indoctrinate the young adults into our generation. Rather, we let them teach us what it is like to live in their world, to feel some of their feelings, and think some of their thoughts. In this way, young adults can better identify with mentors and leaders today.

I recently listened to a young lady, a senior in high school, talk in gripping detail about a three-night hiking trip she and her uncle embarked upon in July. Although it was summertime on the Grand Teton, an abundance of snow and ice covered the upper elevations where they were hiking. Unfortunately, there was so much snow they lost sight of their trail on the second day. As the sun went down, it became colder, and without a clear path, she quickly became exhausted and overwhelmed with fear, thinking to herself they were lost. Her story became even more vivid as they made their way down the mountain. They did not see other hikers, and they had no way to call for help. She trusted her uncle and his proficiency in navigation, which kept her moving one step at a time even though her legs were tightening. They decided to deviate from their original plan and take a different path, eventually leading them to a safe place and a successful ending of their hike. To this day, Ellie compliments her uncle Grayson on his keen discernment, guidance, and leadership.

Many factors embedded within this story could be explored at length—the different path, trust, wisdom, courage, and all the other elements surrounding the two hikers trying to find their way. The questions of life and death were ever present. Pertaining to spiritual mentors, the young disciple identified her uncle as what Barna refers to as a "faith champion." In this spirit, his guidance, discernment, and leadership provided an intergenerational relationship they will forever treasure.[6]

We need not climb the Grand Teton to be considered faith champions. We can, however, climb emotional, intellectual, and spiritual mountains with our young people by supporting them through spiritual mentoring. Think of Paul. Think Timothy. "Continue in what you have learned and firmly believed, knowing from whom you learned it and how from childhood you have known the sacred writings that are able to instruct you for salvation through faith in Christ Jesus" (2 Timothy 3:14-15). By speaking into the lives of young adults and helping them develop their gifts, strengths, and competencies, remarkable connections occur not simply for a day, but for a lifetime. With this encouragement in mind, researchers Kinnaman and Matlock urge us to realize the crucial role of mentors. Their data and surveys show "intergenerational relationships are central to the concepts we've been describing, and these kinds of relationships don't usually happen by accident. They require intentional planning and consistent effort from everyone involved."[7] The youth will learn to lead as they have been led.

The early Christian community certainly learned from James the importance of his mentoring, and throughout the world, they began leading in the way they had been led. From the oral tradition to the words of John's Gospel, we see the source for this leadership in Jesus who says, "I AM the good shepherd" (John 10:11 emphasis added). This "I AM" metaphor and passage will open us to the promise of leadership. It is here we find the reward not in a gold watch at retirement, but the satisfaction of knowing we sacrificed for the next generation.

THE GOOD SHEPHERD

I'll never forget when on sabbatical, my wife and I were able to travel to Israel. The sights, sounds, names, and places all made the Bible come alive in ways I had only imagined. I recall one afternoon in particular on the lower slope of the Mount of Olives where we prayed at the Garden of Gethsemane. The tourist is treated to spectacular views of Jerusalem from this vantage point, but I was less interested in photo opportunities and more focused on the images and sights that touched my soul within.

As we walked down the valley, standing opposite the looming Temple Mount, the guide pointed out we were in the Valley of Jehoshaphat. The name of the valley was not familiar to me, but the guide informed us that from the time of the prophet Joel this valley has been identified as the location where the nations will assemble before God for the last judgment. Thus, it is called "Jehoshaphat," meaning Jehovah has judged.

The guide then explained the valley is also known as the Kidron Valley. My ears perked up when I made the connection. Jesus no doubt walked through the valley where we now stood as he left the Garden of Gethsemane and was taken back to Jerusalem for his trial and judgment. The guide then slowly read the twenty-third psalm, "Yea, though I walk through the valley of the shadow of death" (Psalm 23:4 KJV). At that moment, no tourist could ever take a picture or imagine what was going on inside of me. The Kidron Valley, the valley of the shadow of death, "for thou art with me," the reality of Jesus walking this walk, all came alive within me in a way I will forever cherish.

I think of King David when he was a boy and had wrestled with a bear and a lion. With God's strength, he feared no evil. Although everyone around him laughed, David told Saul he feared no evil as he was prepared to take on the evil found in the giant Goliath. We know the story of the slingshot, and we know the story of the cross. But what holds both stories together, in a way that became crystal clear when I stood in the valley of death, is that our faith fears no evil. David begins his twenty-third psalm with the remarkable words, "The Lord is my Shepherd." This image of God as our shepherd is fulfilled in the Gospel of John where we hear Jesus announce, "I am the good shepherd." (John 10:11)

Jesus is the shepherd of our souls. His rod comforts us and protects us so we fear no evil. His staff pulls us to safety and rescues us when in we are danger, so again we fear no evil. The imagery of the shepherd further comes alive in John's gospel for all who hear the voice of Jesus, and who are quick to listen and slow to speak. But for those who are angry, for those who would not listen, they only pick up stones to hurl at the shepherd and shout blasphemy. (John 10:33)

There in the valley—in the valley of the shadow of death—we picture Jesus carrying his cross and giving his life, knowing "no one takes it from me, but I lay it down of my own accord. I have power to lay it down, and I have power to take it up again. I have received this command from my Father" (John 10: 18).

Jesus leads as he has been led by the Father. As we walk with this next generation and follow James by being "quick to listen, slow to speak, slow to anger" (James 1:19), we may travel through the valley of death, but we fear no evil. And we lead, just as we have been led.

CHAPTER SUMMARY

- The requirement for becoming a Christian was something new to consider, and the early basic beliefs of Christianity all set the foundation upon which the church would stand. Cohesion and agreement were necessary. So, too, was leadership.
- We see James exercising his leadership publicly at the Jerusalem Council. He reminds the church to be "quick to listen, slow to speak, slow to anger" (James 1:19). This is good advice for any leader but especially the Christian who by nature respects the dignity and the image of God in each person.
- Listening leads to patience, which is a form of love. Leadership helps define reality and by following the model of James the church offers a different emotional climate for developing community life.

- Jesus is the Good Shepherd which speaks into his style of leadership. He is the shepherd of our souls, and his rod comforts us and his staff rescues us even though we may walk through the valley of the shadow of death—we fear no evil.

A Talents Inventory

Directions: On the graph on the next page, place a ✓ for each talent you possess in column 1. Then ask yourself whether any volunteer work you are doing now utilizes that particular skill and indicate in column 2. Thinking about PREVIOUS volunteering—were you asked to use this skill? Indicate yes with a [check symbol] in column 3. Then in the final column indicate whether or not this is a skill you ENJOY using. You can write in additional talents you possess, not listed, in the blank rows at the bottom.

TALENT INVENTORY

Talent	Possess It?	Using Now?	Used in Past?	Enjoy It?
Oral communications				
Written communication				
Artistic skills				
Relationally gifted (good people skills)				
Organizational ability				
Attentiveness to detail				
Creative/ inventive				
Good at planning				
Good at making things (e.g., sewing)				
Know how to repair things				
Counseling skills				
Being intuitive				
Being persuasive				
Teaching				
Visualizing				
Problem solving				
Math skills				
Computer skills				
Research skills				

Analysis				
Good at making decisions				
Leadership abilities				
Capable of inspiring/ motivating others				
Athletic skills				
Nursing skills				
Accounting skills/knowledge (e.g., tax prep)				
Knowledge of the law				
Know how to write a business plan				
Musical talent				
Speak another language besides English				
Good typist				
Good listener				
I could teach someone how to drive				

Reprinted with the permission of Vocationalstewardship. org © Amy L. Sherman, 2011

CHAPTER 11

DISCERNMENT

"WELCOME WITH MEEKNESS THE IMPLANTED WORD" (JAMES 1:21)

We come to the final story recorded in Scripture that pertains to James. Obviously, this does not end our consideration of James since we are still reflecting on his life and witness today, and his message will undoubtedly engage future generations as well. In addition to the Bible, collections of writings and letters about James exist, some of which were found in the treasures of Nag Hammadi, Egypt, in 1945. Other historical documents have been handed down to us as tradition developed from the early church and preserved by historians and the church fathers.

Our attention, then, intentionally turns to Luke's account of the early apostles, as we reach his apparent eyewitness account in the closing chapters of the Acts of the Apostles. Luke uses the second person plural "we" through this final section, which encourages the readers to focus more closely on these closing events. In one sense, Luke provides an ominous foreshadowing of what is to come by telling the story of a prophet named Agabus. While prophesizing, Agabus symbolically takes Paul's belt and wraps it around his own feet and hands saying, "Thus says the Holy Spirit, 'This is the way the Jews in

Jerusalem will bind the man who owns this belt and will hand him over to the Gentiles.'" (Acts 21:11)

In one sense, certainly, Agabus casts a foreboding prophecy for Paul. The idea of martyrdom and a violent end should Paul venture to Jerusalem would act as a deterrent for most people from any consideration of traveling. But Paul, having now completed three missionary journeys and anticipating a fourth, was in no mood to stop. Over the years, he had been flogged, stoned, shackled, and imprisoned numerous times, often waiting only for the sentence of death, which always seemed imminent. This prophecy by Agabus appears no different. Although urged by his followers not to go up to Jerusalem, Paul replies, "What are you doing, weeping and breaking my heart? For I am ready not only to be bound but even to die in Jerusalem for the name of the Lord Jesus" (Acts 21:13). The prophecy poses a concern for Paul, but he is far more concerned about not going up to Jerusalem. The matter requires discernment.

Paul knows the risks of witnessing for the faith of the risen Lord—the Messiah—the Savior—Jesus Christ. He is willing to give his life. But his experience teaches him the value found in spiritual discernment. During his missionary journeys, Paul confronted mobs, was embroiled in riots, and faced inevitable conflict when he preached the good news. His beliefs were not always accepted. But Paul had a greater vision. He speaks often of Christ crucified. He knew well such a message was folly for some. But he also feels certain that with the cross comes the resurrection, a new life both available and eternal.

Paul understands his life resides in Christ. Such an existence does not end. Life in Christ can never be taken away. He writes God "is the source of your life in Christ Jesus, who became for us wisdom from God, and righteousness and sanctification" (I Corinthians 1: 30). As a result, this wisdom of God and Paul's vision for life in Christ, means even martyrdom cannot stop Paul. Notice how wisdom and truth work together and provide for Paul the gift of discernment. Through his association with James and Peter over the years, Paul is no doubt familiar with the prophecy by the risen Lord who foretold Peter:

> Very truly I tell you, when you were younger, you used to fasten your own belt and to go wherever you wished. But when you grow old, you will stretch out your hands, and someone else will fasten a belt around you and take you where you do not wish to go. (He said this to indicate the kind of death by which he would glorify God.)" After this he said to him, "Follow me." (John 21:18-19)

PAUL AND JAMES MEET AGAIN

As we follow Paul's decision to continue visiting Jerusalem, our first impression is not one of danger but almost the opposite. Luke records, "The brothers welcomed us warmly." (Acts 21:17) This sense of hospitality, a source of encouragement for Paul's missionary journeys, surely provides a good sign. Perhaps the rift between Jew and Gentile, evident through an earlier account in Antioch (Galatians 2:11), is now beginning to heal. An important indication of this apparent unity is also documented when the next day, Paul meets with James and all the elders. This seemingly small fact may not appear worthy of attention—especially since much of the interest now focuses on Paul—yet Luke documents the presence of James by name as a clear sign of James's leadership within the early church.

We find the ensuing conversation with Paul and James and certain elders fascinating in that both Jews and Gentiles are apparenwtly reporting a win/win situation where all seems well. Paul clearly emphasizes what God has been doing through his missionary work to the Gentiles. He reports not only positive results but significant conversions in Christ and the power of salvation taking place throughout the world. According to Paul, the believers are not only Gentiles but Jews. Paul sees no rift between the Jew and Gentile. Instead, he addresses his obedience and his agreement with all the Jerusalem church has asked of him. Paul's message is working.

When James and the elders hear Paul's report, "they praised God" (Acts 21:20), but they wanted clarification regarding a rumor that Paul's success may not actually be a work of God. According to the word on the street, Paul encourages a relaxation or even worse an abdication of the Mosaic Law (Acts 21:20). And the complaint goes further as they tell Paul the people in Jerusalem believe "you teach all the Jews living among the Gentiles to forsake Moses" (Acts 21:21).

These were not simply scandalous charges or gossip articulated by a crazed mob. Here James and the elders lay out for Paul, a clear case made by the opponents of Paul. The serious charges could bring Paul to trial. A guilty verdict could lead to his death. Obviously, the tenor of the conversation turned sour over this report. Like a dark cloud, the prophecy made by Agabus now covers the room. When such a prophecy meets reality, the outcome seems certain.

Interpretations vary as to what happens next. Some say James turns his back on Paul, leaving Paul to defend himself. Others view this incident as further indication of the separation taking place between the Jerusalem Church and the Gentiles and, eventually, between the Eastern church and the Western church. In other words, what might be taking place at this time in the early church development is a schism. Such a separation appears to further divide the church when it comes to the matter of salvation. The church has argued for centuries whether or not salvation comes by faith as according to Paul, or by works as witnessed by James. Rather than view this as a scene where lines are being drawn, consider this conflict as a need for spiritual discernment.

DISCERNMENT ACCORDING TO JAMES

Discernment is a loaded word. By its nature, discernment literally means to separate or cut. However, we can also understand it as an important spiritual discipline or resource used to distinguish right from wrong, true from false, and so forth. Discernment, by its very nature, is necessary when matters become polarized or when we find ourselves cornered into making binary choices. Discernment helps us bridge the gap and explore not only alternatives and the potential for third and fourth ways but guides us into simply taking the next best step on the journey as we follow Jesus Christ. So, with another powerful metaphor, James writes:

> No one, when tempted, should say, "I am being tempted by God"; for God cannot be tempted by evil and he himself tempts no one. But one is tempted by one's own desire, being lured and enticed by it; then, when that desire has conceived, it gives birth to sin, and that sin, when it is fully grown, gives birth to death. Do not be deceived, my beloved. (James 1:13-16)

Watch the sequence of this metaphor as the imagery takes us from childbirth to maturation. James also adds the component of sin as "desire," which lures and entices, as with an adulterous relationship, and we picture in our mind a seductress who conceives an illicit union. Unintended, destructive consequences occur when desire runs its course. Sin produces death, not life. James then warns Christians who are in the throes of struggling with temptation to be careful.[1] One way of being careful is through spiritual discernment.

In a sense, this imagery of the seductress James offers derives from the wisdom found in Proverbs of the loose woman. She is loud and ignorant and calls to those who pass by, offering them sweet stolen water and pleasant bread eaten in secret. We get the gist. Such a sexual invitation is more than folly or satisfying desire. It is dangerous and illicit. But in the event, we do not get the subtlety, Proverbs clarifies the point, warning such deceit is deadly as her "guests are in the depths of Sheol" (Proverbs 9: 13-18). This imagery contrasts in Proverbs with wisdom where "happy is the one who listens to me. For whoever finds me finds life and obtains favor from the Lord" (Proverbs 8:34-35).

The choice and the consequences seem simple and clear-cut. But life is not always that compartmentalized, and boundaries are not necessarily neatly drawn. Choices overload us today, not just in reference to illicit sex but in something as basic as which cereal to buy, or what to eat for lunch, or what to wear. Seriously, we are pulled in many directions with many distractions at a pace and speed that often confuses us and can make life seem crazy.

But you know, this is no different from the Gentiles who say to themselves, 'What will we eat?' or 'What will we drink?' or 'What will we wear?' In the Sermon on the Mount, Jesus tells his followers "Do not worry about your life, what you will eat or what you will drink, or your body, what you will wear. Is not life more than food, and the body more than clothing?" (Matthew 6:25).

This matter of discernment for Jesus, as for James, is about concerning ourselves with what is important. In other words, it is not the distractions or the unimportant matters of life—of which we find a plethora of everyday examples. Both Jesus and James want us to make healthy decisions by keeping our attention on what is of value—purpose and meaning in life. To that end, Jesus calls upon us to "strive first for the kingdom of God and his righteousness, and all these things will be given to you as well" (Matthew 6:33). Discernment is fundamentally spiritual.

Furthermore, in making decisions about the right thing to do in a given situation and discerning what is of spiritual importance, we are called upon first to pray. Jesus experiences discernment in prayer as does James. When James makes reference to temptation, he sets it within the imagery of the seductress. In the Lord's Prayer, Jesus imprints upon his disciples and followers that behind temptation lies the tempter, the devil. Temptation then is cast upon an even larger spiritual screen of good versus evil. Rather than leave God out of our struggle with temptation and sin and ultimately death, the Lord's Prayer calls upon God to deliver us, spare us, and rescue us and "do not bring us to the time of trial" (Mathew 6:13).

James discerns this potential for conflict in Jerusalem is real. Paul has a target on his back. To move in a healthy, constructive direction, James and the elders tell Paul to join four men and go through the public rite of purification. Some might view this request as punishment. Paul knew from his experience in Cenchreae (Acts 18:18) when leaving Greece after his second missionary journey, the rite of purification was an act of submission, surrender, and letting go. And it is an act of consecration, making sacred the path on which we now travel.

Interestingly, the opening prayer in the Episcopal service for Holy Eucharist is a prayer of purity. Although composed of only a few brief phrases, which does not take seven days for our participation in this rite, the prayer is spoken as we begin our first day of the week, the Sabbath. The prayer of purification casts a vision, establishing, and literally grounding us on the path we are about to take. The prayer says:

> Almighty God, unto whom all hearts are open, all desires known, and from whom no secrets are hid: Cleanse the thoughts of our hearts by the inspiration of thy Holy Spirit, that we may perfectly love thee, and worthily magnify thy holy Name; through Jesus Christ our Lord.[2]

Following the counsel of James and the elders, Paul enters the temple, and he makes public the rite of purification according to the days and sacrifices made for him. There is more to the story of Paul in Jerusalem, but we hear no more from James. Again, some think the silence and apparent absence of James somehow undermines his support of Paul. Yet with discernment, we do not always have the last word. We leave ourselves in the hands of God, which is where we leave Paul, James, and the elders in Jerusalem.

Building spiritual muscles for cultural discernment is essential, especially as we turn our attention to the next generation, as they balance their digital world with the kingdom of God.

I AM THE RESURRECTION

Of the many issues facing the next generation, one concern is the existential anxiety based on getting it right. Just because we have instantaneous access to information, it does not mean the information is correct. In researching questions that have to with school, jobs, finances, or even intimate relationships, we cannot always find answers on a smartphone. It is not about an algorithm. It is more about wisdom.

Discernment is always on the lookout for wisdom and truth, which are of ultimate importance when it comes to matters of faith. If we do not, in our heart of hearts, believe our faith to be true, we find ourselves holding onto something that is false. And false beliefs lead to a false way of living and, ultimately, to living a lie. Here again, we take the importance of discernment and the critical need for the wisdom of spiritual mentors and churches into this consideration of faith. We find mentors essential to help lead this next generation into learning and thinking with wisdom about their understanding of God and a biblical worldview.

This perspective includes a framework for the church—a framework of the creation, fall, judgment, redemption, and restoration working in our lives today. For this next generation, the internet has become the primary educator, and the question Barna Researchers ask:

> How can we live in a deeper, truer narrative about ourselves, about our world, about God's nature and his design for a flourishing human life? Simply put, we can't live in times of complexity without wisdom, the human capacity to understand life from God's perspective—or, to put it another way, a practical understanding of how to live as God designed us.[3]

Such wisdom identifies the need for cultural discernment and the calling for spiritual mentors who are equipped and reinforced by a strong Christian education program that will help the next generation with both thinking and believing in a digital world. Through spiritual discernment, clarity will rise above confusion.

Of course, nothing brought greater clarity to the early church than the resurrection of Jesus. In the Gospel of John, we once again find an I AM statement made by Jesus that was not only unforgettable but became part of the oral tradition that was implanted into the heart and soul of every Christian.

We recall the story as John tells it, when Lazarus became ill, and Mary and Martha sent the request for Jesus to come. Rather than responding immediately, Jesus waited two days longer. When Jesus finally arrived, Lazarus had been dead and in the tomb for four days. Although there is certainly much more to the story, what we need to hear again and again, is Jesus saying to Martha "I am the resurrection and the life" (John 11:25). That is all we need.

Lazarus is raised from the dead. Martha makes her confession of belief. The disciples struggle and are confused as to whether Lazarus was asleep or dead. These concerns equate to the difference between walking during the day and the night. The story is loaded with points of entry, not the least being a plot to kill Jesus following his raising Lazarus to life. Recall, however, James calling the church to "rid yourselves of all sordidness and rank growth of wickedness, and welcome with meekness the implanted word that has power to save your souls" (James 1:21).

The counsel from James is clear and straightforward. First, we are to empty ourselves of the mental garbage and misinformation and all the distractions that have led us astray—the ugliness and growth of wickedness that once planted within us can take on life of its own. Uproot it. Remove it. James makes this point—the destructive side of life will harm and weaken us. All this is part of discernment.

Once we have done an inner-house cleaning or better yet, once the soil has been tilled and fertilized, then we find room for the word of resurrection to be implanted. This imagery speaks to the importance of new birth—being born from above—but it also illustrates the understanding of growth and development made manifest through our new life in Christ. By welcoming with meekness the implanted word, we create hospitality, space, and room for the word to take root within us.

This change or transformation requires spiritual discernment. We need to know what to keep and what to rid ourselves of. We go through a process of sorting and sifting. It takes time. But watch what happens. As we allow the word to be welcomed within, and as we encourage it through the growth in our spiritual discernment process, we find that in time we are capable—in all humility and meekness—of doing the word. To this understanding of doing the word, and to the power it has to save our souls, we now turn our attention.

CHAPTER SUMMARY

- Discernment is a loaded word in and of itself. By its nature, discernment literally means to separate or cut. It is, however, an important spiritual discipline to distinguish right from wrong, true from false, and so forth. Discernment guides us into taking the next best step on the journey as we follow Jesus Christ.

- Paul used discernment when considering the prophecy of Agabus who told him not to go to Jerusalem. The prophecy was a concern. Of greater concern would be not going to Jerusalem and meeting with the church leaders. The Gentiles worried about their lives and the choices before them. James relied on spiritual discernment when making decisions.

- Submission begins the discernment process, and James counsels the church to first "rid yourselves of all sordidness and rank growth of wickedness, and welcome with meekness the implanted word that has power to save your souls" (James 1:21). The Word is implanted and grows within us.

- By his incarnation, Jesus is the Word made flesh and speaks the word, "I AM the resurrection" (John 11:25 emphasis added), which provides us with both the resource of spiritual discernment and the gift of faith in him to live a full and abundant life.

A SPIRITUAL EXERCISE

Henri Nouwen writes, "Discernment is a type of faithful living and listening that ascertains and affirms the unique way God's love and direction are manifested so that we can know God's will and fulfill our individual calling and mission."[4]

Can you speak to how you have learned to live and listen faithfully to better discern God's activity in your life? List several ways you will continue the path you are on and ways you will discern your vocation and direction.

CHAPTER 12

RESTORATION

"BE DOERS OF THE WORD NOT MERELY HEARERS"

(JAMES 1:22)

When I was a child, our family summer vacation always began a with a drive that would test the hardiest of souls. Sitting in a car without air conditioning and no such thing seat belts, I often jockeyed for space with my brothers in the back seat as we bounced around the hilly, hairpin back roads of south-central Kentucky. The trip seemed like an interminable drive from Chicago through the boring flatlands of Indiana to the last several hours in Kentucky when the going really got tough.

What often caught my attention during these trips, and inevitably gave me something to think about during the final long, grueling hours, were crosses strategically placed at the apex of the curve in the road. With tires screeching, oncoming traffic honking, and my father resorting to his Navy days of cussing, those of us in the backseat felt vulnerable as we looked out our windows at a cross that said something like "Are you prepared to die?" or another cross would have the simple question, "Heaven or Hell?"

Children in my day were supposed to be silent. As I sat in the backseat of the car on the highway to who-knows-where, I wasn't about to ask my father who was cussing like a sailor, or my mother who was sitting in stone-cold silence, if I was prepared to die or where I was going. To be truthful, I didn't want to know. Interestingly, by the time I went to seminary and could have asked for answers to those eternal questions, though they were not exactly avoided, I never found satisfying answers. The Episcopal Church at the time was more focused on prayerbook revision. If I heard it once, I heard it a million times, baptism was all that was needed. Baptism was the entrance rite. The waters of baptism seemed to cover a multitude of sins. This understanding of baptism was then woven throughout our liturgical and sacramental theology, and naturally became part of our teaching and preaching.

I bring up these anecdotal stories because now, at my current age and stage in life, I realize these eternal questions are serious and require a mature response. Am I prepared to die? Heaven or hell? I think the sawdust tent and the revival preacher or the vested, liturgical priest in the cathedral both have something in common with Paul and James, especially when it comes to this matter of salvation. Salvation is a gift given to us by God in Jesus Christ. This saving gift can be revealed when encountering the reality of the soul.

HE RESTORES MY SOUL

In beginning, this discussion on the weighty matters of both the soul and salvation, the familiar verse from the twenty-third psalm "he restores my soul" (Psalm 23:3) is a good place to start. I also want to confess from the get-go, the idea of "saving souls" was not part of my early ministry. As years went by, time and again I saw defeated souls, ruined souls, battered souls within the parish. As the need kept growing, I became profoundly aware of the priority for caring and nurturing the soul.

Our culture and academic world seem to have little patience with serious thought given to the soul. Sure,

Hollywood likes the soul as long as it sells. Same with Wall Street, Madison Avenue, and Silicon Valley. Even in Washington, DC, politicians fight, so they say, for "America's soul." Unfortunately, most professions, including politicians, find it difficult to clarify what is meant by the soul. Don't get me wrong, the "soul" is popular. Countless books work the soul into the title or topic, but usually it has little to with God and everything to do with one's self.

With this bleak spiritual landscape today, the acknowledgment and emphasis of the soul in the center of the Christian church needs serious attention. Some years ago, on the fourth Sunday in Advent, I led a Sunday school class discussion on spiritual formation, and the matter of the soul came up. The class wanted to know more. I could tell they were hungry for a discussion. Before responding, I wanted to buy some time, so I turned the question back and asked them what they knew about the soul. Silence followed. Finally, someone said it is an "out of body experience." Many agreed with a nod of approval. Another member said, "the soul takes you to heaven." More agreement. Still others described finding their soul in nature.

As I collected my thoughts, I was aware many thought of the soul only at the time of death. I believe the soul brings life. I reminded the class that just moments before, we'd participated in worship and enjoyed a beautiful Christmas concert and reading of lessons. Everyone wholeheartedly agreed. I then said, "The soul is like our choir director or conductor." Immediately, the class was back on track as was our discussion about the soul. They knew what the choir would have sounded like without a choir director or the instrumentalists without a conductor. At best, the concert would have sounded unpleasant, and at worst, we would have heard chaos and a cacophony of noise. Life without a soul is much like a concert without a director or conductor.

The soul gives the body direction, meaning, and purpose and is vital to the well-being of the body and the heart and mind. No separation or dualism exists between the body and the soul. Our feelings, thoughts, ideas, and our actions all interrelate within the soul. As a result, the soul adds value and significance to life. Without the soul, we would experience a lifestyle that is insignificant and meaningless, without purpose or direction. A life detached from the soul is conflicted and terribly confused, and not far removed from becoming self-destructive. A soul that is harmed, beaten, or lost is, in a sense, polluted. And such a sick state of a soul does irreparable damage to a life that is misled and on a ruinous course. On a more positive note, for a soul that has a good conductor or director, a healthy, disciplined, and vibrant life ensues. A soul restored by God results in blessings that abound.

THE SOUL YEARNS FOR SALVATION

Turn now for a moment, from the brief discussion of the soul to our primal need for salvation. The discussion on "saving souls" turns serious. To say Jesus is my "savior" says just that. He saves me. He saves me from sin and all that separates me from God. The destructive, chaotic, misguided aspects of life that wage war on the soul find a savior in Jesus who provides defense, strength, and purpose to live a new life with God. Jesus refers to this as the "abundant life" (John 10:10). A savior is obviously necessary and essential for our salvation. No savior. No salvation.

Salvation in Jesus opens us to the presence of the kingdom of God where our Savior reigns as King of kings and Lord of lords. And since we are saved, life as we once knew it no longer remains the same. We are different. We have changed. We are transformed by our new life in Christ. Joy, peace, hope, love, and all the spiritual gifts that flow out of the kingdom provides the soul daily with a vibrancy for life now with God—here on earth just as it is in heaven. Life is not about luck or serendipity. Our life now exists for God.

In other words, being saved is ongoing and a lived experience. The Greek word, *sōzō* means both heal and save. Yes, Jesus is my savior. But I can also affirm Jesus is my healer. This is an important consideration, especially when introducing the word sanctification. To say that "I have been saved" and then live as if my life were no different denies sanctification. The soul longs for both sanctification and healing. Healing is a form of restoration. We are restored to new life in Christ. We celebrate the *sanctity* in life. The *Sanctus* is our liturgical way of identifying the holiness of our life with God. A *sanctuary* is where we worship that which is holy. Be assured, our eternal destiny is in the kingdom of God, and this assurance directs and conducts our lives, so they become consistent with and under the obedience of our Lord and Savior, Jesus Christ, whom we worship in "Spirit and truth" (John 4:24) Through the spirit of the Lord, the prophet Isaiah experienced the holy *sanctifier,* and envisioned our growing "like oaks of righteousness" (Isaiah 61:3) called the "Holy People" (62:12).

Hold these thoughts as we synthesize and integrate this understanding Paul has of justification by faith, as compared to James who speaks of being justified by works and doing the word. This brings together the soul, salvation, justification, and sanctification in a way that bears witness to the next generation.

SALVATION AND JUSTIFICATION

Some scholars today focus a great deal of attention on a sharp division or split between James and Paul. They use different accounts of the Jerusalem Council and the letter to the church of Antioch to highlight James as a disciplinarian and Paul as a man of grace. Still others direct attention to James and the Jerusalem Church as witnesses to the Jews, while Paul receives full permission to proselytize and win over the Gentiles. From a theological perspective, however, the division between James and Paul seems to be even greater especially when it comes to the matter of salvation. Paul speaks to salvation by faith. James, on the other hand, says clearly salvation is witnessed in our works. On paper, it appears like the two are polar opposites. Some even see this as the beginning separation between the Eastern and Western church.

Far be it from me to take on two thousand years of church history and theology in one paragraph, but I think we can summarize a few of the basic texts that reveal their similarities in both thought and practice.

Often, a superficial look and reading of the texts in question seem to pit James as the one who rejects justification or salvation by faith alone:

> What good is it, my brothers and sisters, if you say you have faith but do not have works? Can faith save you? If a brother or sister is naked and lacks daily food, and one of you says to them, 'Go in peace, keep warm and eat your fill' and yet you do not supply their bodily needs, what good is that? So faith by itself, if it has no works, is dead. (James 2:14-17)

It appears James could not be any clearer. When he refers to faith without works being "dead" it seems as if he has made his point. In the south we might say, faith without works is as "useful as a screen door on a submarine." Same point as James, only perhaps a bit more illustrative. Yet, in all seriousness, matters like salvation, justification, faith, and works are profound and give purpose for life. Although we may want to pick sides and choose between Paul and James, we can understand matters better by recalling that these early church leaders were writing letters to specific needs for specific churches in a specific time.

Paul seems to exclude works as the basis for salvation because his complete letter makes it apparent God's grace is the most important work. Salvation is ultimately a result of the Lord's work on the cross and not our deeds. If our deeds were capable of saving us, then our faith in Jesus would be weakened, and we would only boast about our actions and the works we perform and not the redeeming work of God. Paul is not contradicting James.

James is concerned as well with weak faith. He sees the hypocrisy of those who claim they have faith (James 2:14) but do not reveal it in their lives. Put this way, faith that is in your head or even on your lips but not carried through in action, signifies a hollow pursuit—a faith that only talks but does not act. Such a faith bears no fruit. Actually, it gets worse as James goes so far to write, "Even the demons believe" (James 2:19).

Both James and Paul address the matter of the Law. Unlike a legalist, Paul knows the Law will not save, while James is like the psalmist who "delights in the law of the Lord" (Psalm 1:2). Both balance the extremes of their day, and they complement one another in their understanding of faith. James writes, "can a fig tree yield olives?" (James 3:12). Faith is like a tree or the root of our being, and as a result of faith, good fruit or good works are produced. If the root is no good, there will be no fruit. James knows this. Paul writes a similar message comparing the works of the flesh to the fruit of the spirit. (Galatians 5).

Below are examples of Paul and James writing that appears as if they are in conflict.

Paul	James
A person is justified by faith apart from prescribed by the law. (Romans 3:28)	A person is justified by works and not by faith alone. (James 2:24)
By grace you have been through faith ... not the result of works. (Ephesians 2:8-9)	So faith by itself, if it has no works, is dead. (James 2:17)

In comparing the texts above, the key word is "justification." In chapter four, we discussed the Greek word, *logizomai,* which refers to being justified or reckoned. *Logos* (Greek) for "word" and central to this meaning of being justified, is most eloquently revealed in the prologue of John's gospel where in Jesus, "the Word (*logos*) became flesh and dwelt among us" (John 1:14). James says this word is "implanted" in us like a seed (James 1:21) and grows by faith, producing good works. Through this word, *logos,* both James and Paul understand the process of salvation and justification by encouraging us to be "doers of the word and not merely hearers who deceive themselves" (James 1:22) or as Paul writes, "love is the fulfilling of the law" (Romans 13:10).

In Christ, the word is made flesh or the incarnate word. Both James and Paul agree as we stand both justified and sanctified, or safe and sound. This expression of "safe and sound" comes from a nautical term. A ship that pulls into harbor with broken machinery or torn sails may have arrived safely but not sound. The ship needs repairs and may stay a long time in dry dock. Theologian, A.H. Strong continues with this illustration of the ship by concluding justification makes the ship safe, but it is sanctification that gives soundness.[1] The growth and development of our life in Christ may take a long time, but the process of salvation leads us to the sanctification of life in Christ and the gift of holiness found daily.

Righteousness and holiness are additional words we need not shy away from as we come to the close of our reflection on the witness of James. In fact, I introduce these words into our spiritual vocabulary knowing James was often referred to as "James the Righteous." These words "righteous" and "holy" are sometimes used within a negative context today. People will scoff and say something like "When did she become so holy?" or "What makes him so self-righteous?" To James, the words holy and righteous are synonymous with being functional. A holy person is a functional person. And Paul refers to the holiness in his writing with the metaphor "if the root is holy, then the branches also are holy" (Romans 11:16), which speaks both to faith and works. For both James and Paul, faith is the root. Works are the fruit. No root: no fruit. No fruit: no root.

In our day, it is common to use the word "dysfunctional" to describe a characteristic. This is where restoration is required, and again both Paul and James bear witness to a life of salvation that gets the job done through the work of mentoring that restores the image of God.

MENTORING FOR RESTORATION

We can move forward in our "doing the word" and living a life of restoration through spiritual mentoring. We have discussed this concept throughout this book as a practical outcome for the church and the next generation in experiencing spiritual growth through the witness of James.

As I look over my years in the parish ministry, I notice now I was being both called and led every decade into a varied and yet deepening experience of spiritual mentoring. In the latter part of the 1980s, I was rector of a large Episcopal parish and ran nonstop. During this time, I participated in a three-year extension program on spiritual direction through the Shalem Institute for Spiritual Direction in Washington, DC.

I was placed in a small peer group with members who were likewise engaged in spiritual mentoring. We were placed under personal spiritual direction as well, and since I was from Kentucky, the nearby Abbey of Gethsemane was perfect for me to locate a director. In addition, I began to provide parishioners with insight and guidance for both individuals and groups. I think it was helpful for those I met, and I know it certainly blessed me.

I thought I was set for life, and then we experienced growth in the parish with an expanded capital building program and doubled our staff. I did not give up on my spiritual growth, but, in retrospect, I saw the need to change my leadership style and take a deeper look at developing my administration abilities. I had never thought of administration as "ad-ministry." But through the work and training of a two-year program in Ministry Coaching International, I found myself still providing spiritual direction—only now mentoring on a different platform. I cared for the staff and the assortment of presenting issues in a way that seemed to fit the gifts I now claimed. The integration of faith and works became an ongoing reality.

One final example coincided with the turn of the century. Through prayer and discernment, I began working on a marriage mentoring program. One of my sons was preparing for marriage. No way could I conduct any premarital counseling with him and his bride-to-be. The idea of turning my son and future daughter-in-law over to a mature couple in our parish sounded intriguing. We developed a series of training sessions under the leadership of Harriet and Mike McManus and their Marriage Savers ministries. The mentoring program made an immediate and personal impact. Now ten years later, my daughter-in-law and son still look back at their mentors as two wonderful Christian people who came into their lives at just the right time. Remarkably, they all still keep in touch and watch as the next generation, our grandchildren, grow.

I share these personal stories with you at the end of this book not to walk down memory lane but to illustrate the need and the importance of mentoring and the variety of shapes and styles it takes. We will not find a cookie-cutter, one-size fits all design for mentoring because we are unique. Mentors come with distinctive gifts, skills, and competencies. You are one of a kind.

With that said, all mentors hold together and leverage a deep, faithful opportunity for communication with the next generation concerning vocation that is at the heart of our conversation. Helping young adults, as they begin their pilgrimage into adulthood with an everlasting communion of all the saints, is an untold blessing as they identify with the characteristics and attributes of all the saints. As mentors, we provide the witness and the model for restoring the faith community and our mission to a world in desperate need.

I hope you will notice the "Dedication" of my book is to our grandchildren. They are near and dear to our hearts, and if I can provide a listening ear or be of counsel to any of them, there is nothing that will hold me back. Trust me, we need grandparents as mentors for the next generation. The call is not to throw in the towel on what is ahead but rather to restore and pay attention to these dear souls who are growing up around us. They need you. They need God. For a stronger church tomorrow, I hope you will listen to the call for spiritual mentors that has been extended throughout this book.

The first spiritual mentor for the church was from a long time ago in a place far, far away. I am referring not to Obi-Wan Kenobi imparting his wisdom to a young Luke Skywalker in his battle with the dark side. But unlike the stuff of Hollywood, we are in this time and this place for real. James writes to the church and to mentors from every generation "If any of you is lacking in wisdom, ask God, who gives to all generously and ungrudgingly, and it will be given to you" (James 1:5). Heed these words. God saves us by faith alone, but James is the first to tell us God will never, ever leaves us alone. Through the witness of James, we are called to mentor a new generation of resilient disciples who have both the spirit and the will to be "doers of the word." It is the word of God for the people of God.

A Spiritual Exercise:

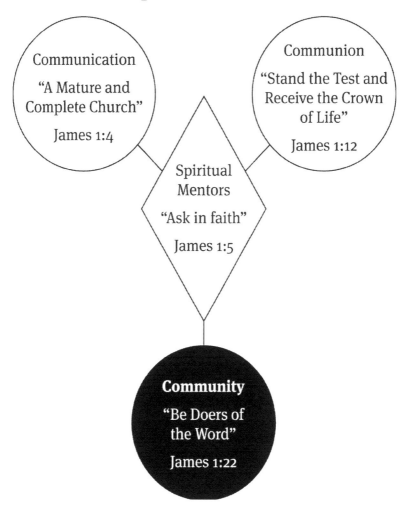

Scripture reminds us "Where there is no guidance, a nation falls, but in an abundance of counselors there is safety" (Proverbs 11:14). We end our reflection with this reminder which offers hope. Mentors provide a forward path that holds a blessing. There is safety in the mentor, but more importantly, there is salvation in the gospel.

This is where we end the book but begin by doing the word.

AFTERWORD

An Interview with Theresa Wilson

Theresa Wilson is former director of the Nashville Fellows Program of the Fellows Initiative. She and her husband Clint are the parents of one son, James. Following her husband's recent call as rector to St. Francis in the Fields, they now live in Harrods Creek, (Louisville) Kentucky. This interview came from questions by the author while writing this book. For further information about the Fellows Initiative visit: <u>www.thefellowsinitiative.org</u>

(RTJ) Theresa, thank you for your time this morning. I have a few questions about the Fellows Initiative and its church-based programs—actually ministries—how they work and why they are important for the church and the next generation.

(TW) You are right, they are ministries and are volunteer driven. And what better place than the church. The group of Fellows programs across the country are all part of the Fellows Initiative and began with the Rev. John Yates in Falls Church, Virginia. John saw the need for these programs when he encountered college graduates coming out of school with degrees and uncertain what to do with their education and how to launch the next phase in life. The Fellows programs are designed to provide a holistic offering for the development of young adults. Yes, they are firmly rooted in the local church. We provide mentoring in discerning a vocation that equips Fellows in responding to God's call on their lives. It is a model for leadership and discipleship for emerging adults who want a good start and to start well as faithful Christians. The transition from college to adult living is a critical period and we are here, as caring Christians, to help them navigate.

(RTJ) So, does this mean seminary or entering into the ordination process?

(TW) It's possible. But for most of the participants, they know the year after college is an important passage in their life, and Fellows programs provide an opportunity to hunker-down and reflect with a peer group and mentors on how to apply their faith to work. So many people think of work as drudgery or a pain, and they can't wait until Friday for time-off to do what they really want to do. As a result, we have it backwards in our culture and in the workplace. God created us for work (Gen. 1:28, 2:15). Our job is to redeem or restore work to an original purpose, be it law or teaching or manufacturing. Understanding our purpose on earth and what God has in mind for us is life changing. Applying our faith to all of our life is what the church is about.

(RTJ) It sounds exciting but also a bit overwhelming. Will you say more about the model? Where do these young adults come from? What is expected of them?

(TW) It is exciting! All Fellows Programs are rooted in local churches, so the Fellows have a spiritual home in a new city right away. They live with a family from the church for nine months, which is the length of the program (August-May). They are assigned a mentor and are expected to be mentors—using the Timothy biblical model. Volunteer work in the church is required as youth leaders, through which they lead small groups and mentor youth. They also have a day set aside for reading, reflecting, and participating in a seminary level course on Christ and culture, a Bible overview, and the theology of work. This isn't necessarily ivory tower, because they meet with city and corporate leaders who give them a vision for what it means to celebrate the good *and* redeem the broken parts of their industries within their city. There is also time set aside once a week where they gather and make dinner. Time is given to discuss their faith journey, and, in the spring, we focus on how their faith informs various relevant topics. Again, the main components are a professional job with commensurate pay in their field of interest, seminary level coursework, personalized mentoring, service and support in the church, an incredible network in the city, and a peer group who become lifelong friends.

(RTJ) Sign me up!

(TW) We will as Louisville is ripe for such an offering. There is a, however, a cost, and it's important for sponsoring churches to raise the necessary funds in advance for a Fellows Program to launch. Also, preparation time is needed to identify a cadre of community leaders who will have positions available for work, mentors, and welcoming homes. This advance work is the key to success of our programs around the country where screening takes place of the program: the church leadership, mentors, homes, corporate leaders, and the applicants themselves go through an intensive interviewing process. It is hard work and prayer.

(RTJ) But it is a blessing—correct?

(TW) Absolutely! I can't say enough how these young adults at the end of the year are light years ahead of their peers in terms of self-awareness, a network in a new community that would take most adults ten years to create, and best of all, a church that has blessed them, so they in turn can be a blessing to others.

ABOUT THE AUTHOR

The Rev. Robin Jennings enjoyed a lifetime of pastoral experience as an ordained Episcopal minister and rector of St. Francis in the Fields, Harrods Creek (Louisville) Kentucky. As an accomplished author, speaker, and teacher, his spiritual insights into everyday life experiences bring both practical help and a deepening hope. His timely topics include the power found in the vision for our life with God, the ongoing need for renewal of the mind, and the importance of giving witness to the next generation. All of these topics are richly woven into his speaking and are the basis for his three-volume book series on spiritual growth.

Named as one of the top religious leaders by *Louisville Magazine*, Robin currently serves on several non-profit boards in Louisville, and he is a member of the Kentucky Speakers Association. When not engaged in speaking or writing, Robin and his wife, Mary, love travel and taking church groups on pilgrimages. They have been blessed with four sons (one of whom is deceased), three lovely daughters-in-law, and six wonderful grandchildren who receive their full attention when they are home. And then there is the family dog, Knoxy. Robin can be reached at: www.robintjennings.com

Robin would appreciate you posting a short review on Amazon, Barnes & Noble, and Goodreads. Reviews mean the world to an author.

ENDNOTES

Introduction

1. Fr. John-Julian, OJN "The Martyrs of Memphis 1873-1878" excerpted for September 9, from: *Stars in a Dark World: Stories of the Saints and Hold Days of the Liturgy,* Outskirts Press, England 2009.

2. David Kinnaman & Mark Matlock, *Faith for Exiles: 5 Ways for a New Generation to Follow Jesus in Digital Babylon.* (Grand Rapids, MI. Baker Books, 2019), 214.

3. Ibid., 34-35.

Part One

1. Jerry Sittser, *The Will of God as a Way of Life* (Grand Rapids, MI. Zondervan, 2004), 168.

2. David Kinnaman & Mark Matlock, *Faith for Exiles: 5 Ways for a New Generation to Follow Jesus in Digital Babylon* (Grand Rapids, MI. Baker Books, 2019), 146.

Chapter One

1. Robert Eiseman, *James the Brother of Jesus: The Key to Unlocking the Secrets of Early Christianity and the Dead Sea Scrolls* (New York, NY Penguin Books, 1997), 415.

2. David Kinnaman & Mark Matlock, *Faith for Exiles: 5 Ways for a New Generation to Follow Jesus in Digital Babylon,* (Grand Rapids, MI. Baker Books, 2019), 71.

3. David Kinnaman, *You Lost Me. Why Young Christians Are Leaving Church…and Rethinking Faith"* (Grand Rapids, MI. 2011), 30.

4. Keith Anderson and Randy Reese, *Spiritual Mentoring,* Intervarsity Press, 1999

Chapter Two

1. Scot McKnight, *Kingdom Conspiracy: Returning to the Radical Mission of the Local Church* (Grand Rapids, MI. Brazos Press, 2016), 142.

2. Ibid, 128.

Chapter Three

1. Scott McKnight, *Kingdom Conspiracy: Returning to the Radical Mission of the Local Church* (Grand Rapids, MI. Brazos Press, 2016), 128.

2. Lillian Tryon, D.N.P. *"Biblical Concepts of Restoration as a Foundation for Lifestyle Change"* The Journal of Biblical Foundations of Faith and Learning: Vol.3:Issue1, Article 28. 2018. p. 7.

Chapter Four

1. C. FitzSimmons Allison, *Guilt, Anger & God* (Vancouver B.C. Regent College Publishing, 2003), 46.

2. Douglas J. Moo *James* Tyndale New Testament Commentaries, vol. 16 (Downers Grove, Ill. InterVarsity Press, USA second edition, 2015), 50.

3. Ronald J. Sider *Rich Christians in an Age of Hunger: Moving from Affluence to Generosity* (Nashville, TN. W Publishing Group, Division of Thomas Nelson Publishers, 1997, 5th ed.), 21.

4. David Kinnaman and Gabe Lyons, *UnChristian: What a New Generation Really Thinks About Christianity...and Why It Matters* (Grand Rapids, MI. Baker Books, 2007), 40

5. David Kinnaman. *You Lost Me. Why Young Christians Are Leaving Church...And Rethinking Faith* (Grand Rapids, MI. Baker Books, 2011), 207.

Part Two

1. Scot McKnight, *Kingdom Conspiracy: Returning to the Radical Mission of the Local Church,* (Grand Rapids, MI. Brazos Press, 2014), 102-3.

2. David Kinnaman & Mark Matlock, *Faith for Exiles: 5 Ways for a New Generation to Follow Jesus in Digital Babylon* (Grand Rapids, MI. Baker Books, 2019), 33.

Chapter Five

1. *The Voice of the Martyrs*, "Nepal: When Family is the Enemy" (Bartlesville, OK. October 2020), p. 4

2. David Kinnaman and Gabe Lyons, *Unchristian: What a New Generation Really Thinks About Christianity...And Why It Matters* (Grand Rapids, MI. Baker Books, 2007), 40.

3. Tim Elmore, *Artificial Maturity: Helping Kids Meet The Challenge of Becoming Adults* (San Francisco, CA. Jossey-Bass, 2012), p. 4.

4. Teresa of Avila, *Interior Castle,* the Classic Text with a Spiritual Commentary by Dennis J. Billy, C.Ss.R. Ave Maria Press, Notre Dame, IN. 2007. P. 41.

5. David Kinnaman and Gabe Lyons, *"UnChristian: What a New Generation Really Thinks About Christianity...And Why It Matters."* (Grand Rapids, MI. Baker Books, 2007), 180.

6. Douglas J. Moo, *James* Tyndale New Testament Commentaries, vol. 16. (Downers Grove, Ill. InterVarsity Press, USA. Second edition, 2015), 49.

Chapter Six

1. Dave Kinnanman, *You Lost Me: Why Young Christians Are Leaving Church...And Rethinking Faith* (Grand Rapids, MI. Baker Books, 2011), 171.

2. Ibid., 212.

Chapter Seven

1. Dallas Willard, *Knowing Christ Today: Why We Can Trust Spiritual Knowledge* (New York, NY. HarperCollins Publishers, 2009), 54.

2. David Kinnaman & Mark Matlock, *Faith for Exiles: 5 Ways for a New Generation to Follow Jesus in Digital Babylon* (Grand Rapids, MI. Baker Books, 2019), 180.

3. David Kinnaman and Gabe Lyons, *Unchristian: What a New Generation Really Thinks About Christianity...and Why It, Matters* (Grand Rapids, MI. Baker Books Publisher, 2007), 46.

Chapter Eight

1. AARP Foundation and United Health Foundation, "The Pandemic Effect: A Social Isolation Report" October 6, 2020. P. 4

2. Rodney Stark, "The Rise of Christianity: How the Obscure, Marginal Jesus Movement Became the Dominant Religious Force in the Western World in a Few Centuries" (New York, NY. HarperOne edition published by arrangement with Princeton University Press, 1997), 167.

3. David Kinnaman & Mark Matlock, *Faith for Exiles: 5 Ways for a New Generation to Follow Jesus in Digital Babylon* (Grand Rapids, MI. Baker Books, 2019), 194.

4. *The Book of Common Prayer*, (New York, Church Publishing Incorporated, 1979), 364.

5. David Kinnaman & Mark Matlock, *Faith for Exiles: 5 Ways for a New Generation to Follow Jesus in Digital Babylon* (Grand Rapids, MI. Baker Books, 2019), 180.

6. Ibid., 192

Chapter Nine

1. John Painter, *Just James,* (Minneapolis, MN. Fortress Press, 1999), 60.

2. David Kinnaman & Mark Matlock, *Faith for Exiles: 5 Ways for a New Generation to Follow Jesus in Digital Babylon* (Grand Rapids, MI. Baker Books, 2019), 147.

3. Ibid., 113

Part Three

1. Steven Garber, *The Fabric of Faithfulness: Weaving Together Belief and Behavior,* (Downers Grove, Ill. InterVarsity Press, 2007), 159-160

2. David Kinnaman & David Matlock, *Faith for Exiles: 5 Ways for a New Generation to Follow Jesus in Digital Babylon* (Grand Rapids, MI. Baker Books, 2019), 114.

Chapter Ten

1. Dietrich Bonhoeffer, *Life Together* (New York: Harper & Row, 1952), 97.

2. Max DePree, *Leadership is an Art* (New York: Doubleday, 1989), p. 9.

3. David Kinnaman & Mark Matlock, *Faith for Exiles: 5 Ways for a New Generation to Follow Jesus in Digital Babylon* (Grand Rapids, MI. Baker Books, 2019), 125.

4. Ibid., 127.

5. Ibid., 140

6. This story was used by permission and was first recorded at St. Francis in the Fields Episcopal Church, Harrods Creek, Kentucky, February 7, 2021 within the context of Youth Sunday.

7. Ibid., 139

Chapter Eleven

1. Douglas J. Moo, *James* Tyndale New Testament Commentaries, vol. 16. (Downers Grove, Ill. InterVarsity Press, USA. Second edition, 2015), 100.

2. *The Book of Common Prayer*, (New York, Church Publishing Incorporated, 1979), 323.

3 David Kinnaman & Mark Matlock, *Faith for Exiles: 5 Ways for a New Generation to Follow Jesus in Digital Babylon* (Grand Rapids, MI. Baker Books, 2019), 81, 84

4. Henri Nouwen with Michael J. Christensen and Rebecca J. Laid, *Discernment: Reading the Signs of Daily Life* (New York, NY. HarperCollins Publisher, 2013) 163.

Chapter Twelve

1. A.H. Strong, *Systematic Theology* (Valley Forge, PA. Judson Press, 1993), 869.

FOR FURTHER READING

I enjoyed writing this book as I often felt surrounded and supported by a company of saints, a cloud of witnesses, and many authors. Yet, recommending reading material to another person is a bit like me choosing paint colors for your living room. May I suggest you pick and choose, and if you should select one of these books, you do the research and make sure it fits your needs.

Reading today is a sacrifice. Authors are working harder than ever to catch your attention. Handheld phones have taken over. I get it. I'm still old school, and a book is a book. I like to read, reflect, save words, underline, highlight paragraphs, and hold on to books that speak to me. Consider this list then as "nothing but joy" (James 1:2).

JAMES

Moo, Douglas J. *James*: *Tyndale New Testament Commentaries*. Downers Grove, IL: InterVarsity Press, USA. 2015.

Motyer, J.A, *The Message of James*: *The Bible Speaks Today Series*. Downers Grove, IL: InterVarsity Press, USA. 1985.

Painter, John. *Just James: The Brother of Jesus in History and Tradition*. Minneapolis, MN: Fortress Press, 1999.

Tabor, James D. *The Jesus Dynasty: The Hidden History of Jesus, His Royal Family, and the Birth of Christianity*. New York, NY: Simon & Schuster, 2006.

Tabor, James D. *Paul and Jesus: How the Apostle Transformed Christianity*. New York, NY: Simon & Schuster, 2012.

Bütz, Jeffrey J. *The Brother of Jesus: and the Lost Teachings of Christianity*. Rochester, VT: Inner Traditions, 2005.

Bruno, Chris. *Paul vs. James: What We've Been Missing in the Faith and Works Debate*. Chicago, IL: Moody Press, 2019.

THE NEXT GENERATION

Kinnaman, David & Lyons, George. *UnChristian: What A New Generation Really Thinks About Christianity...And Why It Matters*. Grand Rapids, MI: Baker Books, 2007.

Barna, George & Kinnaman, David,.*Churchless: Understanding Today's Unchurched and How to Connect with Them*. Carol Stream, IL: Tyndale Publishers, 2014.

Kinnaman, David. *You Lost Me: Why Young Christians Are Leaving Church ... And Rethinking Faith*. Grand Rapids, MI: Baker Books, 2011.

Kinnaman, David & Matlock, Mark. *Faith for Exiles: 5 Ways for a New Generation to Follow Jesus in Digital Babylon*. Grand Rapids, MI: Baker Books,2019.

Lyons, Gabe. *The Next Christians: Seven Ways You Can Live the Gospel and Restore The World*. New York, NY: Multnomah Press, 2010.

SPIRITUAL MENTORING

Anderson, Keith R. & Reese, Randy D., *Spiritual Mentoring: A Guide for Seeking and Giving Direction*. Downers Grove, IL: InterVarsity Press, 1999.

Horsfall, Tony. *Mentoring for Spiritual Growth: Sharing the Journey of Faith*. Abington, United Kingdom: Bible Reading Fellowship, 2008.

Horsfall, Tony. *Mentoring Conversations: 30 key topics to explore together*, Abingdon, United Kingdom: Bible Reading Fellowship, 2020.

Sellner, Edward C. *Mentoring: The Ministry of Spiritual Kinship*. Cambridge, MA: Cowley Publications, 2002.

Kettler, Peter S. *Life on Life: The Practice of Spiritual Mentoring*. Meadville, PA: Christian Faith Publishing, 2018.

SPIRITUAL FORMATION

McKnight, Scot. *Kingdom Conspiracy: Returning to the Radical Mission of the Local Church. Grand Rapids, MI: Brazos Press, 2014.*

Sherman, Amy L *Kingdom Calling: Vocational Stewardship for the Common Good.* Downers Grove, IL: InterVarsity Press, 2011.

Willard, Dallas. *Renovation of the Heart: Putting on the Character of Christ.* Colorado Springs, CO: NavPress, 2002.

Willard, Dallas. *The Divine Conspiracy: Rediscovering Our Hidden Life in God.* San Francisco, CA: HarperSanFrancisco, 1998.

Nouwen, Henri with Christensen, Michael J. and Rebecca J. Laird, *Discernment: Reading the Signs of Daily Life.* New York, NY: HarperOne Publishers. 2013.

Wright, N.T. *After You Believe: Why Christian Character Matters.* New York, NY: HarperOne Publishers, 2010.

Garber, Steven. *The Fabric of Faithfulness: Weaving Together Belief and Behavior.* Downers Grove, IL: InterVarsity Press, 2007.

AVAILABLE FROM
ROBIN T. JENNINGS

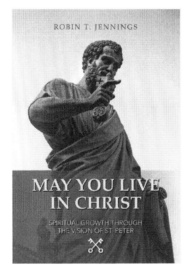

Cast a vision for a new you. If there ever was a model for us and for living in this fast-paced world of ours, it is in the life of St. Peter. If Jesus can transform this impulsive, conflicted, vacillating man into the greatest of our saints, then surely there is hope for you and me.

"Thank you so much for sharing the beautiful reflection on St. Peter in, *May You Live in Christ*. I read it last evening with delight and personal benefit."
—The Most Reverend Joseph E. Kurtz, D.D., Archbishop of Louisville, Kentucky

ALSO AVAILABLE FROM ROBIN T. JENNINGS

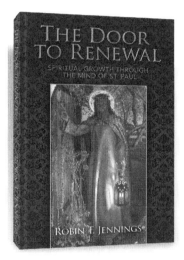

Are You Ready?
For Christians seeking a personal journey of renewal, this book will encourage you to learn from St. Paul's witness and use it as a framework to help you: learn from his conversion, his profound conversation within the kingdom of God, and his eternal convictions.

"Robin takes a heartfelt practical look at some of the most challenging issues that life offers up, and yet he helps the reader understand how they can apply the principles of godly living to their own situation."
—Simon Barnes, Former Executive VP, American Bible Society Bath, England

Made in the USA
Columbia, SC
18 November 2021